MW01005390

THE RECTOR AND THE VESTRY
THE ESSENTIAL GUIDE FOR THE ANGLICAN CHURCH

"*The Rector and the Vestry* is a goldmine of great counsel, practical advice, background explanations, personal anecdotes, and sound teaching that I highly recommend. I plan to use it for my Vestry every year."

—The Rev. Alan Hawkins, COO,
ANGLICAN CHURCH IN NORTH AMERICA

"I came into the Anglican Church from a parachurch / Evangelical background. There were reliable books and guides to help me learn Anglican History, Sacramental Theology, and the Book of Common Prayer. There was nothing that helped me grapple with the unspoken assumptions that governed the roles of the Rector and the Vestry. I am grateful to the Rev. Canon David Roseberry for his friendship over the years and this vital resource. It is the fruit of decades of leadership in the local church combined with a keen, broad awareness of the issues facing Anglican Churches today. I am privileged to serve a congregation where many have a similar story to my own. I plan on reading through this with our Vestry and future Vestry candidates to help us see how the Rector and the Vestry work well together to support our broader mission."

—The Rev. Daniel Adkinson,
ST. THOMAS ANGLICAN CHURCH, ATHENS, GEORGIA

"As a church planter, I've been looking for the information in this book for years. What a resource! The wisdom and practical advice that David Roseberry distills from his years of ministry is invaluable. Every church planter, every rector, and every vestry member needs this book. Thank you for writing this book, David! It's a gift to the Church and I will be using it as my vestry training manual from now on."

—The Rev. John G. Wallace
RECTOR, APOSTLES BY-THE-SEA ANGLICAN CHURCH
IN ROSEMARY BEACH, FLORIDA

"Receiving and reading your manuscript has been a 'God send' for me. It has answered many questions and clarified confusion regarding my roles and responsibilities as both a member of the St. James Vestry and as Senior Warden. What a blessing (and I hope a benefit to the rector and congregation) that I am reading this at the beginning of my term."

—David Chapman
NEWLY APPOINTED SR. WARDEN,
ST. JAMES, COSTA MESA, CA

The

RECTOR

&THE VESTRY

THE ESSENTIAL GUIDE
FOR THE ANGLICAN CHURCH

WRITTEN BY THE REV. DAVID H. ROSEBERRY
EXECUTIVE DIRECTOR, LEADERWORKS

An Anglican Compass Book
An Imprint of LeaderWorks

The Rector and the Vestry: *A Very Essential Companion and Guide for the Rectors, Wardens and Members of the Anglican Vestries*

© 2020 by Rev. David H. Roseberry

ISBN
Paperback 978-1-7343079-4-8
Ebook 978-1-7343079-5-5

Text and Cover Design by Blu Design Concepts

1. Anglican 2. Vestry 3. Rector 4. Guidebook

ANGLICAN COMPASS
7200 Dallas Parkway, Suite 1022, Plano, TX 75024

Published in the United States of America

To Jed: I am so proud to see the faithful man, husband, father, son and pastor that you have become.

ACKNOWLEDGEMENTS

I AM THANKFUL for so many people who took part in developing and writing this book. The Rev. Daniel Adkinson, my former priest-associate and Vicar at Christ Church, was a writing partner. He did some of the early research for this book. The Revs. John Wallace, Brian Pape, Andrew Petta, and Al Zadig are all Rectors and read the manuscript in earlier versions and made many helpful comments and suggestions. The Rev. Canon Phil Ashey, the Provincial Canon Lawyer for the ACNA, looked over the chapters on the Canons and made very wise points for me to clarify and correct. I am thankful for three Senior Wardens (Ron Bosher, Chris Lipper, and David Chapman) who encouraged me to press on with this. My friend and literary coach/agent, Bruce Barbour, was a mid-wife for this work.

My favorite part of the book was writing about the 27 Senior Wardens who came to dinner at my home. I wrote it with tears in my eyes and with a full and thankful heart for all of them. They were like the people of Christ Church: endlessly patient with me as I learned to lead over 31 years as Rector.

And I am most thankful for my devoted and loving Fran who constantly encouraged me to write this book for the benefit of future clergy, vestries, and congregations who care about the Gospel of Jesus Christ. She read the entire work and urged me on.

TABLE OF CONTENTS

INTRODUCTION

I WORK WITH CHURCHES and the leaders that lead them. And I love it. In the past few years I have met some amazing leaders and passionate kingdom-minded workers. These brothers and sisters in Christ work hard to move their church forward on mission. The leaders I have met are smart, eager, and faithful. The Rectors are, for me, especially impressive. Many of them could have had very successful careers in a more lucrative profession. Indeed, some of them had careers that were headed that way; they left the business world, went to seminary, got ordained, and started new congregations. Many new leaders have been called to lead existing churches and are faithful in bringing their best thinking and energy to the task. I think the Anglican Church in North America has more than their fair share of these leaders.

Other leaders are working in congregations that are not new at all. They have been transplanted from a prior denomination. They face their own unique set of challenges. Some have never missed a beat. They have gone from strength to strength. Some congregations still have endless litigation to contend with. Some churches have ministry that is in need of revitalization or renewal. These churches come in all sizes and ages; many are small and attempting to grow and expand their footprint. Some are waiting for the next Rector or Vicar to come and lead them.

These churches, leaders, laypeople, pastors, and people love the Lord Jesus and are committed to the effective life-changing proclamation of the Gospel and the administration of the Sacraments of the church.

While it is impossible to uniquely characterize all of these different churches, every one of them have at least three things in common. First, there is a Bishop who is responsible to oversee the vitality of the work. The word "bishop" itself is derived from the New Testament word for "overseer." Each of these churches has a leader who is typically an ordained priest. The word "priest" is derived from the Greek word for "elder" or "presbyter." The priest may be a man or a woman; our Province has both in these ordained roles. And each of these congregations has a Vestry or some other named group of lay people, elected, appointed, or assigned, who are helpers and leaders in the congregation.

The Vestry, or whatever that group of laypeople is called in your church, is an integral part of the Anglican way of leading and developing congregations. Vestries are not incidental to the life of the church. But neither are they the focus of the life of the church. Vestries serve the church and its mission in service to Jesus Christ as its Lord. The idea of having a Vestry of lay members of the church is common to all Anglican congregations.

What is NOT common at all is a clear understanding about what a Vestry is supposed to do. Many people who are currently serving on a Vestry, or who have been nominated to serve, are new to the Anglican Church. Some may never have heard of a Vestry. The average person in the pews or chairs can figure out what a bishop is, who his Bishop is, and what he is for. The same is true for the role of Rector or leader in a church. People are familiar with that duty. But many people who are deeply committed Christians and ardent worship attenders, even those who are cradle Anglicans, do not really understand the role and responsibilities of a Vestry in a congregation.

The goal of this book is to describe the role of the Vestry at a comprehensive level. I hope this will be helpful to those who are considering serving or who have been elected to serve on a Vestry. I offer this book in the hopes that there can be a common understanding of what a Vestry is equipped and canonically capable of doing. Serving on a Vestry for a typical three-year term is not an honorary position. It is, and should be, ministry. It is an important ministry and is needed now more than ever.

If you are on a Vestry or are considering serving in this capacity, I hope you will read this book cover to cover. There are no unimportant aspects to the role of Vestry. Your experience and your gifts, time, efforts, prayer, and energy can make a critical difference to your church. That is my belief and my hope. And, as you understand the import of this ministry, I know it will strengthen your church and increase your faith in Jesus Christ. I hope that every chapter and every page will help you help your church fulfill its mission.

Your Church Vestry

There is a reason why a book like this is needed today that may not be apparent to you at first. Many of our clergy and parishioners in the ACNA come from other ecclesial backgrounds or no Christian background at all. Consider the Vestry in your church right now. Here is a random list of people who might be serving as members of your Vestry:

- Bill is a mature Christian who came into your church from a Bible Church background and understands what an Elder Board is. He has been the head of one a few years back.

- Mary, Phil, and Frank all have Methodist backgrounds. They know all about committees and how they are supposed to report back to the board.

- Tom's wife nominated him, and he was easily elected. He has never served on a church board, but he is the popular chairman of a local non-profit. He brings that experience to the Vestry.

- Marcie is a new Christian and is excited to serve the Lord this way. She is a very active volunteer in the Youth program and wants the youth to be represented.

- Kevin is a Nigerian-born immigrant who was very active in his Anglican Church outside of Lagos, Nigeria. He attended a parish in England during his graduate studies there. Now he attends the church and is known as a very friendly usher.

- Fr. Steve is the new young Rector who is only a few years out of seminary. He was called to bring a youthfulness into the parish. He has a Young Life background from a large Presbyterian congregation in another part of the country.

Do you see the challenge that awaits a Vestry as diverse as this? There are multiple experiences of church governance on your Vestry right now. If our efforts in evangelism and outreach are successful, this will be even more true in the years to come. And, with this diversity in mind, it is easy to see how a Vestry might struggle to understand the correct and best role for itself.

Put simply, this book is written to assist and empower every Vestry and Rector to be as unified, effective, and focused as they can be.

Who Are You?

As I mentioned above, this book is written for several audiences.

It is written for the Rector and Vestry of a church to distribute among their current Vestry and nominees. Oftentimes it will take months, if not close to a year, for elected Vestry members to "get the hang of it." After three decades of forming and leading vestries, I would often hear from the outgoing class, "I am so glad that I served on this Vestry. I have seen God move in our church…and in me!"

It is written for so-called "Rookie Anglicans" who have been nominated to serve or who just want to know how their local parish works. One of the great things that is happening in our denomination is the influx of those who have discovered the Anglican Way in their adult years. This is even true of our ordained leaders. Anglican Polity has clear implications for every church, and those who are new to the Anglican Way could greatly benefit from a book like this.

It is written for the Rector of the congregation who is looking for something that he or she can use to develop a stronger team of leaders on the Vestry. The Rector of your congregation is my hero. I love the work that Rectors do, and for many years, I shared in the burden-bearing that they undertake. I wrote this book for them. Rectors will be the final "gate-keeper" for how the Vestry operates, subject to the leadership of the Bishop. But I hope the Rector of your congregation will be empowered and strengthened to attempt greater things for God and do them!

It is written also for the Bishops of the Anglican Church in North America. They are godly men who are forging ahead building our new Province. Most of them were Rectors at one time; some of them still are. They have led their fair share of Vestry meetings in their own parishes. Since it is the role of the Bishop to develop a culture of governance and strength for the churches under his pastoral care. I hope this book will be a useful tool in that process.

A Word about Your Church

I cared deeply about Christ Church in Plano, Texas when I served as Rector; we had a great run of 31 years. But I also had great times of teaching, preaching, consulting, and helping other congregations thrive. Over these years I came to see that each congregation, yours included, is a unique organism in its own right. Your church is a family of faith, a collection of unique members and unique memories of God's incredible faithfulness in times past and present.

Wise leaders should remember that patterns of work and participation on a Vestry are established over time. Essential elements and a particular style and culture are built over long periods of time, leadership, prayer, and good will. Vestries are an ecosystem of styles, roles, past leaders, and year-by-year functions. Even young churches have established ways of doing things. These are called traditions, and traditions in a congregation make quick changes in style, culture, or substance sometimes very difficult. Leaders should show great care and respect for how things got to be the way they are.

I stepped away from my role as Rector of my former parish to enter a new phase in my life and ministry. I heard a call from God to do it. The clarity of God's call to release this ministry was surprising to me. In effect, God said, "It's time." I obeyed as best I knew how.

And then God began to show me how I could begin a Non-Profit Foundation called LeaderWorks to help strengthen and encourage leaders and the parishes in the Anglican Church in North America (ACNA). Primarily, my ministry involves teaching and training pastors and Rectors, working with them and their congregations to do the work God has called them to do in their missionary context. After several years working with many groups, I am more convinced than ever that the key to the strength of our Anglican movement is healthy churches led by trained and equipped Rectors working with strong teams to do the work of ministry.

I: INTRODUCTION

I am so pleased to offer this book for your use. I do not see this book as a final edition for your church. The more I wrote, the more I realized there was to be written. In other words, by God's Grace, there is more to come. But I do hope this book can be an anchor resource; something that has enough weight and heft to be useful as you need it. And I hope I have written about most of the right topics and most of the topics right. May it serve you well and glorify our Triune God of grace!

In Christ,

The Rev. Canon David H. Roseberry

II. YOUR CHURCH

The Big Picture

DO YOU REALIZE what your congregation is? Do you realize what your community of faith means? Without being too dramatic or overstated, your church is part of a wider group of churches all around the world that comprises the most durable, important, world-changing, self-renewing, mission-driven organization on earth. It is important to keep this fact in mind. If you believe God has a providential plan for the world and all people are under His gracious governorship and rule of our Lord Jesus Christ, then your church is an essential part of the spiritual lives of the people who are its members.

Your church is a critically important way that God calls, leads, and sends His people from one generation to another. There is no other organization on earth with such a high calling and such a clear mission. C. S. Lewis wrote in *Mere Christianity* (Chapter 8),

> *The church exists for nothing else but to draw men into Christ, to make them little Christs. If they are not doing that, all the cathedrals, clergy, missions, sermons, even the Bible itself, are simply a waste of time. God became*

man for no other purpose. It is even doubtful, you know, whether the whole universe was created for any other purpose.

When Jesus gave the Great Commission to the disciples after his resurrection. But he gave it to them as a gathered group. He did not give each one a personal mission to explore and develop their personal understanding of the Gospel on their own. Perhaps you have heard that Christianity is not a spectator sport. That is certainly true. But neither is it a solo performance or an individual effort to live the Christian life. *The Risen Christ gave the Great Commission to a gathered group.* He gave it to <u>them</u>, plural!

A quick survey of New Testament Scriptures will prove the point. Jesus did appear to individual disciples one by one. The Good News of the Resurrection was revealed to a few here and there. However in every case, Jesus holds back the mission until they are all gathered together. When Thomas missed the first revelation of Jesus to the disciples, Jesus did not find him and give him a personal cameo appearance. He waited until the disciples were (again) gathered and showed himself. Even the Apostle Paul, who had the most personal and individualized encounter with Christ of anyone in the New Testament, was immediately led away to a group, a church, to recover and redevelop his thinking. In fact, he was escorted to a place where he could be nurtured and protected, not by secret agents and personal guards, but by the church.

And at the same time, the church became the gathered group of human beings who would come to develop the methods and the means to organize the mission work. And, as we see in the rest of the Gospel, the Book of Acts, and rest of the New Testament letters, the Good News of Jesus Christ came from on high to ordinary men and women who would need to learn to work together for the benefit of the Gospel. And thanks be to God, the Holy Spirit changed them and developed them into world-changers! Indeed, under the influence and guidance of the Holy Spirit, a full-fledged self-sustaining organization would emerge to carry the Gospel forward generation to generation.

This is an amazing fact of the New Testament story. Jesus called fisherman, tax collectors, sinners, and ordinary people to follow him as disciples. Within a generation, these men and women had laid a strong organizational foundation for this growing group of ordinary people to literally change the world. This really is a miracle in and of itself!

Too Big to Fail?

Outside of my apartment window is a massive corporate-sized building. Electronic Data Systems built its world headquarters in Plano, Texas. Their offices stand high above the prairie of North Texas, spreading out over acres of former grassland and cornfields. The building that they built is about 1.6 million square feet of offices, conference rooms, training centers, and personnel support services. It is so massive that it blocks the sunlight into my apartment window for 30 minutes every morning! It is huge! It was built for the future. It was designed to dominate its industry for the next century. Or so it was thought.

Today, the EDS building is empty, and the company is gone. The massive Fortune 500 corporation made a few leadership mistakes and didn't see the shift in business models that the Internet would bring. Imagine that! The data processing king didn't see the future coming. They retracted, downsized, and fell apart. Their monumental achievement, the massive headquarters near my home, is empty. Empty! I am sure that stockholders and corporate leaders thought that EDS was too big to fail. But the current businesses and organizations that we put our faith and trust in are, in fact, just passing through. They will change; they will fade away. But, as Jesus said to his disciples, the church would last unto the ages of ages. Nothing, not even the gates of hell would prevail against it. The church, with all of its challenges, has been pronounced dead on many occasions. But it always renews itself. Century after century, the church continues to go from age to age, from culture to culture, from people to people, from nation to nation. And it changes everything it touches.

The church is the oldest continuously renewing and reforming organization that has ever existed. The oldest company that is still going strong is a furniture maker in Italy. Their family business goes back only 700 years. But the church is 2000 years old! Your congregation, the family of believers with whom you are growing in the faith and learning about our Lord Jesus and His outward mission, your church is on the leading edge of that movement.

This awareness should change the way your church operates. *A church that has its timeless mission in mind can roll over obstacles and setbacks with great momentum.* So, if you are the Rector, an ordained leader, a nominated Vestry candidate, or an elected/appointed member of a Vestry, your role is **NOT** about running the church, building the programs, or raising the funding. Those things are important, and you must attend to them all. However, they are not the mission. You have been ordained, called, chosen, nominated, or elected to be a faithful steward of this God-blessed, Christ-centered, Holy Spirit-empowered, faith-based, longest-lasting, world-changing enterprise.

This is the work you are to do.

III. WHAT IS ANGLICAN POLITY?

NOW WE CAN TURN to some of the details about church governance and the unique way that Anglican churches are led and governed. But in order to do that, I need to introduce you to a phrase that you may never have used, let alone heard: "Ecclesiastical Polity".

First, let's understand what the word "polity" means. It is not used too often in regular street speech. But, as you can see, it has something to do with the word "politics." And a wordsmith would know that the Greek word for city is "polis." Polity is related to all of these and it refers to the way a group of people govern themselves as a community. A "polity" is a set of rules and standards that are agreed upon by the group. And if you see the word "ecclesiastical" ("ecclesia" means the "gathered ones," i.e. the church) in the first position, you have an endlessly interesting subject: Ecclesiastical Polity.

Let me show you how interesting it can be.

A few years ago, while I was leading a Vestry meeting, one of our members asked to make a point about church polity. That alone impressed me. Luke was a skilled attorney in his own practice, but he had been mostly silent in our previous sessions. He didn't say much, but when he did speak, people listened. He observed, *"David, I have been doing some reading on churches and the way they hold property titles and govern themselves. I have come to see there are only two kinds of churches in the world: Congregational and Hierarchical."*

He went on to say that congregational churches are the churches that are self-contained, self-governed, and mostly independent. They are organizations with their own charter, their own by-laws and constitution, and their own governing boards. Some of these congregational churches can even ordain their own ministers. They have their own statement of beliefs or confessional statement. Churches like this may draw upon the help or resources of other churches like them. They can form associations, networks, or even missional relationships in order to do their mission or train leaders. There is no shortage of this kind of church, both large and small.

Then he described the other model for church governance and leadership: the hierarchical church. These churches exist as part of a structured hierarchy. They might appear to be self-governed, but they are subject to the leadership and direction of a hierarchy over them. There is a Bishop or a superintendent or some judicatory in authority that *"oversees"* the work of the church. There are codes of conduct, standards and clear boundaries of belief that hold a family of believers together as a coherent family. The "Seven Sisters" of mainline American Protestant Christianity are typically the most hierarchical churches we have in the USA. They are the United Methodist Church, the Christian Church (Disciples of Christ), the Presbyterian Church, the Episcopal Church, the Evangelical Lutheran Church in America, American Baptist Churches, and the United Church of Christ.

Roman Catholic and Orthodox congregations are also hierarchical with Bishops, Archbishops, and other systems and leaders "above" the congregation.

And here was Luke's point: Congregational and hierarchical churches and their forms of government are as different as night and day. The Congregational model have their own problems, as do those of the Hierarchical model. But, simply put, my friend had it right. Well, almost right. There are indeed only two kinds of churches in the world: congregational and hierarchical. But Anglicanism actually blends the two together to from a third type. Like so many things in the Anglican tradition, there is a third way: the Anglican Way.

The Third Way of Anglicanism
For many reasons, both theological and historical, the Anglican Church in North America (ACNA) is a "blend" of both of these types. In

terms of style, focus, mission, employment of clergy, and incurrence and payment of debts, the ACNA *leans toward congregationalism*. But in terms of accountability, theological beliefs, training and ordination of ordained leaders, worship life, liturgy, and teaching, the ACNA *leans toward the hierarchical form of government*.

In other words, the polity of the Anglican Church in North America is a third way. As we will see, we hold that the local congregation is the basic unit of mission for the Anglican Church. Congregations are charged to make disciples of Jesus Christ on behalf of the Anglican Church. But the congregation secures its own property title, it raises its own budget, and it makes its own decisions about program, mission, and focus. There are no ongoing subsidies that keep the congregations afloat. However, each congregation and each member of the clergy are independent only if they adhere to a basic body of beliefs and practices set by their Bishops. The "higher authorities" in the ACNA (the Bishops) exert an enormous spiritual, moral, persuasive, and mission-defining authority over clergy and congregations. But it is a non-legal authority. The ordained leader and the congregation are free to stay linked into the Province and under their bishop and diocese; they are free to leave the fellowship too. This third way system relies very heavily on the relational strength of a Bishop and the Rector of the congregation.

This "blended" form of governance is the ecclesiastical polity of the ACNA. We rely heavily on the local congregational leader to lead locally AND the regional, diocesan leader to oversee regionally. This is our ecclesiastical polity in a nutshell: *Congregational freedom to engage the mission plus Diocesan oversight to guide and direct the effort.* This is the Anglican Third Way.

We will talk about the role of the Bishop relative to the congregation below, but first let's see how this unique blend of congregational and hierarchical leadership works itself out.

A Common Mission

The mission of the ACNA is to *Reach North America with the Transforming Love of Jesus Christ.* That is a fine mission statement. But, like all mission statements, it needs to be actualized. We need to see it in action. We need to ask *how* this will get done.

Here is the plan: Every church, every congregation, led by the Rector and Vestry, is charged to fulfill this mission. The Constitution and Canons of the ACNA say that the main mission of the church is to be carried out by the local congregation. The Provincial and Diocesan structure serve and empower the congregation as they engage the mission of the church.

But, even though each of the congregations

independently determine how they are going to fulfill the mission, *they are not independent.* Our congregational polity is also hierarchical. There is an ordered, historic relationship between each congregation and their Bishop. There is collaboration and encouragement between congregations (Rector and Vestry) and their Bishops. There are also appropriate canonical checks and balances that govern these systems and relationships.

It is beyond the scope of this book to outline how a diocese governs itself and how the College of Bishops govern themselves. Those topics are for another day. But this blended Anglican polity that we have highlights the serious and central role of the Rector and Vestry in relationship with their Bishop.

Are We a Franchise?

Perhaps an analogy might serve well here. The ACNA Constitution makes it clear that congregations are owners of, and self-contained units for, the mission of the church. Each congregation is the clear owner of their property and all the aspects that that would entail. They also have their own style, if you will. They do their own marketing. They train leaders to work in their own churches. Even if a congregation does not own property (and many do not; they are so new and young), they are still the chief determiners of what they will lease, use, rent, and perhaps, one day own.

III: WHAT IS ANGLICAN POLITY?

Each Anglican congregation must exert an energetic focus, strength, and commitment to become something sustainable. The diocese is not going to take over if the mission stalls in one congregation. In the language of business, the individual congregation is not a "franchise" unit out in the field. They are wholly "owned" by the local board of governance or the Vestry.

But, as mentioned above, there are systems of oversight and relationship that can assure members that the doctrine, disciplines, and worship of the church are being followed.

Further, when it comes to the mission of the ACNA to reach North America with the transforming love of Jesus Christ, each congregation is called to embody this mission as strongly and as clearly as they can. But they are not to do this alone. *They are to remain in partnered fellowship with their Bishop.* Each congregation is called to the good and faithful stewardship of this mission under God, but always as partners with other congregations in the same diocese.

It is a very interesting dynamic that every Vestry member needs to understand and appreciate. It is why every church is expected to contribute time and money to the health and vitality of their own diocese. The church is a local group with a very localized ministry that arises from the heartbeat of the congregation. Yet, at the same time, each congregation is expected to "hold fast" to the Anglican ethos of its diocese.

This is where the canons of the church come in. In a very real way, the way that congregations are linked to their diocese and the diocese to the national province is through an approved set of rules, standards, and written codes of conduct and assumptions. Let's take a quick look at how they functon.

IV. CANONS
AND BY-LAWS

THE WORD "CANON" might be foreign to new members of the Vestry. A "canon" is a rule, or a law. It can be applied to Scripture, as in "the Canon of Scripture" which means the established texts of the Old and New Testaments. It can be applied to a person who is working on behalf of a diocese or in a cathedral, as in "Canon Smith." But most Vestries will want to keep in mind that a "canon" is a certain rule or written code of church law that makes up our "polity" or our way of doing things. "Canon" is not spelled like the ballistic ordinance (cannon), but they are powerful, nonetheless. Church canons are organized by titles and sections that are codified and adopted by a governing board of a diocese or the national church. The diocese has a list of canons, as does the national body of the Anglican Church in North America.[1]

It is instructive to note that congregations do <u>not</u> have canons. They have by-laws and policies that should be printed or available. By-laws typically are minimal descriptions of how an individual congregation is organized and functions internally.

---

1 The ACNA Constitution and Canons are found on their website: AnglicanChurch.net. Most dioceses post their own Constitutions and Canons on their website.

Provincial Canons

With all of this said, there are some canons of the Anglican Church in North America that concern congregations, Rectors, and by extension, Vestries. You will also want to refer to the governance documents of your diocese and the by-laws of your congregation for clarity and local precision. (Remember, since parishes do not have canons, only by-laws, their by-laws are always subject to the canons of the diocese, which in turn, are subject to the canons of the larger province of the ACNA).

(See Appendix 4 for a list of the top canons that every Vestry member should know.)

As we look to the Canons of the ACNA, we begin to see the role and purpose of the local congregation.

For example, Canon 6 of the ACNA asserts the primacy of the local congregation as the fundamental agency of the mission of the Church, reminding us that the chief agents therein are the people of God! Every congregation should be attached to a diocese under the oversight of a Bishop. The canons mandate that each congregation

shall be established in accordance with the laws of the State or jurisdiction where situated, shall handle its own finances, and shall carry insurance coverage in amounts specified by its Diocese.

Canon 6, Section 5, is specifically concerning governing boards and it states:

> *There shall be a governing board of each congregation, often known as the vestry, which is chosen and serves according to applicable laws, diocesan canons, and the congregational by-laws. The Presbyter in charge of the congregation shall always be a member of the governing board and its presiding officer except as provided by diocesan canon. The governing board is responsible for the temporalities of the congregation and, except where otherwise provided by canon, supports the clergy in the spiritual leadership of the congregation.*

Vestry members pay attention!

Notice that the Canons of the Province begin to spell out the high-level detailed purpose of a Vestry or Governing board. We will examine this later in the book, but this canon is a good summary. In terms of leadership, there are legal areas, financial areas, and fiduciary responsibility that need attention in the local congregation. The Vestry gives leadership and attention to these and other areas!

Diocesan Canons

Some diocesan canons may give greater detail to the role of the Rector and the role of the Vestry. For example, the canons of the Anglican Diocese of the South (ADOTS) outline what matters are under the purview of the Vestry.

The Vestry shall be responsible for the management of the Congregation's business affairs, including the following:

- Support of the Rector and his family, including contributions to a retirement plan or pension;

- An adequate place for regular worship;

- The musical program of the congregation, which shall be under the control of the Rector;

- The salaries of all staff members, once determined by the Rector and the Vestry;

- An adequate insurance program for the Rector and staff, and proper insurance to protect all property, real and personal, of the congregation and all persons attending congregational services and functions;

- Compliance with the constitution and canons of the church and of this diocese;

- Establishment of a Biblically based program of financial giving;

- Conformity (as nearly as possible) with the congregation's annual financial commitment made to the diocese;

- Support of the Rector in all aspects of his ministry; and,

- Approval of and compliance with all contracts and other obligations entered into by the congregation.

In the Diocese of the Mid-Atlantic (DOMA)[2] the qualifications and duties for Vestry are listed with less specificity.

The Vestry shall at a minimum have the following duties:

- Provide for the financial support of the Rector and the Rector's family;

- Pray regularly for the Rector, the Rector's family, and the Congregation;

- Support the Rector in all aspects of the Rector's ministry, including ensuring the Christian formation, biblical literacy, and spiritual maturity of the members of the Congregation;

---

2 It is hard not to smile at the explosion of acronyms in the Anglican Church in North America. They create an insider shorthand for many groups and entities in the ACNA: ADOTS, DOMA, C4SO, etc.

- Provide an adequate place for regular worship;

- Provide for the elements necessary for worship and administration of the Sacraments;

- Provide for the compensation of staff members;

- Establish an adequate insurance program for the Congregation that includes, at a minimum, property damage, liability, personal injury, and errors and omissions;

- Support biblically based financial giving by members of the Congregation;

- Share in the financial support of the Diocese; and,

- Strive for unity and adopt the principles found in Matthew 18 as the standard for resolving conflict that may develop within the Vestry, the Congregation, the Diocese, and the Province.

It would be a very worthwhile exercise for your Vestry to fully understand the canonical duties that are associated with its role at the level of your diocesan canons. It is likely that you will find the governing canons of your diocese on the diocesan website. These are important documents to be aware of for your work together.

And again, it should be remembered that the canons of the wider body trump the canons of the smaller body. This means that if there is conflict between the diocesan canons and the parish by-laws, the diocesan canons are observed.

Going back to my friend's observation, the Anglican Way of governance is both congregational AND hierarchical. This is good news for your Vestry and the mission of your congregation. It means that your church is independent to discover a local expression of Christ's mission, but your church is dependent on the linkage to your Bishop and diocesan family. Your church is free to be the congregation that you are called to be or become, but you are not free to do anything you want. There is both local authority in developing your mission AND regional accountability in doing it.

Lanes and Curbs

Let me offer an analogy to explain this. In my small hometown in southern Arizona, there was one road going north and south. Everyone who was going anywhere in that town traveled up and down Grand Avenue. This was a very small town, and when the town council decided to widen Grand Avenue, it was a big deal. They worked on it for years. And when it was done, our family took a drive that evening to ride on the newly paved improvement in our town. That was our fun for the week! We rode north to south and then south to north. It had been widened to include two lanes going north and two lanes going south, as well as a middle lane to turn across traffic. Big time!

It was the driver's choice as to which lane to use going north or south. As long as we kept going the approved direction, we were free to move from one lane to another. But there were limits about how far to one side or the other that we could go. There were limits about where we could turn left or right. There were curbs and curb cuts to allow us to choose our own way within the pattern of traffic that had been designed by wise town fathers.

Canons are like curbs. They form the outside boundaries of what we can do in the church. They will also show us where we can have freedom on the road and where we are pushing our limit of freedom.

I hope this gives us a shared framework and starting place as we think about the role of the Rector and the role of the Vestry. When the Rector and the Vestry have shared expectations and fulfill their roles, and where they are in line with the curbs and Canons, there is harmony and health in the church!

V. WHY CHURCH
SIZE MATTERS

IF WE ARE TO SPEAK honestly and specifically about the role of the Vestry in the life of a congregation, we have to include a topic that is tender to the touch: Size. This is a tender topic in the church today because size is often correlated to impact, effect, success, and strength. Of course, this correlation can be true. But it can also *not* be true. But there is no getting around the fact that a Vestry of a small church is going to have a different role than the Vestry of a large church. I hope to show you why in this chapter.

But first, let me lay out one idea that might make this topic an easier one to discuss. Size and impact are not correlated in the biblical story. We all know that power in the ancient Roman world was centered around Caesar Augustus and the city of Rome. Luke tells us in the Christmas story that, while the powerful politicians in Rome issued decrees and edicts that commanded people to move here and there, one small, nondescript family was relocating at the far eastern corner of the Roman Empire. The birth of Christ almost went unnoticed. Christ was born in a tiny, out-of-the-way village and raised in a hometown that was easily ignored, even ridiculed.

The birth of Jesus was, by worldly standards, entirely forgettable. But a few centuries later, the Christian faith was taking over the world; it has continued to this day. Worldly size and strength are not correlated with impact or outcome in the biblical story.

Yes, size does matter. There is an aspect of the size of church that will cause it to function in a certain way. Actually, it is better said in the reverse: behaving and functioning in a certain way with certain patterns and roles will cause a church to settle or grow into a particular size. It is a version of the famous maxim of the organizational expert Peter Drucker who said, "Culture eats strategy for breakfast!" This means that a Vestry can desire change, hire staff to cause change, strategize for change, and pray for change. But if the culture and people in the church are unwilling to change, change is impossible. Culture always wins.

Personally, I hope that every church could have a full measure of faithfulness and vision. I encourage churches to be what God has called them to be, regardless of their eventual size. But, having said that, we can make a few comments about the size, corresponding culture, and challenge of leadership in a congregation.

Four Sizes of Churches

In my work with many congregations, I have found a helpful illustration to help churches think about church size dynamics.

We can draw some parallels from the education sector to think about how churches of different size function and about the unique leadership dynamics of each size. For purposes of this illustration or typology, I want to consider four unique kinds of schools, their learning environments, their relative size, and their make-up. But I also want to point out distinct patterns and culture found in these four different contexts: The Home School, The Grade School, The High School, and The College Campus. And for each of these contexts, I want to apply some principles to the local church that would correspond to it.

The Home School
Do you know anyone that homeschools their children? There is a distinct dimension of size and culture in that type of learning environment. Learning takes place in a living room or maybe even around a kitchen table. A Home School is a loving learning and training center for children and it also protects them from the challenges of the larger institutions. The Home School is a place of nurture.

Now consider this culture as it would apply to a congregation. The Home School size Church has an average Sunday attendance of about 20-40. Everyone does everything together. The Vestry is elected rather informally and, after a while, all of the adults in this size church are expected to serve on the Vestry. Everyone should have a turn at it. A

Vestry member may be put in charge of a specific church task, the way a family puts together a list of chores for the household. Hopefully, there is great joy and community in this size congregation. The Rector knows everyone and there is access to the Rector in the same way that every student in the Home School can find to the teacher/parent. The Rector's spouse and children are well-involved in this size church.

In a small church like this, a Vestry might meet and talk about last week's lower-than-normal attendance like this: "I know the Smiths and the Garnets were both vacationing this weekend.", says one member. Another says, "Well, Betty has been ill and Wilma has a mother to take care of now. I guess that's why they weren't in church. That's two more families out." The Rector says, "I also heard that Arnold's car broke down on Saturday afternoon. He called me on Sunday to see if I could find a ride for him, but it went straight to voicemail. He was going to bring his four kids, so that is another half-dozen people down."

This size church is going to remind most people in it of a family. Families are great, when you are in them. And people who are new visitors to this church see a group of people who are super-friendly to each other. But these Home School size churches can sometimes seem closed off to outsiders. Entrance into this kind of church takes a long time.

But it is hard not to see the appeal of a Home School size congregation. They are one big happy family (hopefully).

The Grade School

In most communities there are Grade Schools or Elementary Schools for students. The Grade School classroom is much more structured and standardized that the Home School environment. In the classroom there is one teacher and a few assistants who volunteer their time. The single teacher is responsible for all knowledge that is transmitted and permitted in the classroom.

There are churches that correspond to this kind of culture. These churches have about 50 to 80 in attendance. The Rector is the purveyor of information and the organizer of all curriculum. He or she oversees the member's learning and provides instruction appropriate to their age and stage in life. The Rector of the Grade School-size church is most appropriately called "Father." And in this size church, the "Father Knows Best", to remember the old television show. He is the one who always says, in a loud voice, "The Lord be with you" to bring people to attention. All shared meals begin with his prayer. In fact, few meetings or session ever happen without his presence.

This type of learning environment can also be very nurturing. In fact, I can remember the name and the face of every single one of my teachers in grade school. They are imprinted on me. Mrs. Stephens,

Mrs. Flotow, Miss Waddell, and Mr. Ezzo. All of them are in my mind's eye. And to the point, I can remember only a few of my high school teachers.

There are obvious challenges for the sustainability of this size church. And sustainability for this size is a very common problem for many congregations in the ACNA. These churches may have great fellowship and family strength, but they have a hard time growing past the ability of the one leader to be the "Father" for more than 80 people.

Now that you see how the culture of a classroom and a congregation can be similar, let's quickly touch on the remaining two types of congregations. And thankfully, I am going to skip over the Middle School grades because, let's be honest, it was an awkward time that most of us just tried to survive!

The High School

So now, let's think about the next size church category like a high school. This is a church of about 100–200. In this size, the school is not organized around a person. It is organized by subject. Students no longer have one main teacher teaching them most subjects. Instead, they have a team of specialists and teachers. The students have many teachers they can learn from, but they have their favorite teacher too. There is also a broader culture of school spirit, extra-curricular activities, and a clear organizational culture.

The Rectors of a High School size church tend to think of themselves as high school principals in many ways. The Rector here is a leader of leaders. If a science teacher is absent one day from the class-room, you would never expect the principal to teach science that day, or any day. You'd expect the principal to have led the school to develop a system for absentee teachers to find a substitute and provide a daily lesson plan.

Additionally, people usually attend this church not because it has a great Rector who tirelessly tends to his people. They attend the church because they have heard it has a great youth program or missions program. It reaches the community around it by offering ministries and ways that people can be trained, engaged and involved.

The principal is the person who does the hiring and interacting with department heads on the one hand and an administrative board (Vestry) on the other hand. Indeed, the Vestry of this size church feels more like a board of advice and counsel, which is appropriate. In this church there is a greater emphasis on communication and coordination.

The College
Finally, there is the college size church. It might be a smaller college-sized church of 400 to 800 or a large university-size church of 1000 people or more. Churches of this size are their own institution and

THE RECTOR AND THE VESTRY

they are very rare indeed. There are a few of these churches in the ACNA, but only a few.

These churches have their own culture, ethos, and eco-system. They are well known to the broader community and their peers. They have a certain reputation (for better or worse). The Rector leads like a college president with different departments or schools that have their own respective internal structures. A lot of the president's work is with the faculty and governing board. The board is probably a group of alumni and experts that have been recruited or persuaded to serve. The Vestry of a church this size may be similar. Some members will be highly involved. Others simply love and value the church. Still others will bring specific skillsets. The glue that holds the parish of this size together is not only one another (in small groups or class experiences) but also in the large, public events of worship and celebration. The preaching and the music are key reasons why this church is attended by many; even by many who have no other connection point with it.

In this size church you first hear the word "campus." The buildings and facilities receive far more attention at this stage. A college president might be building all the time! They are figuring out what is needed, and which schools/departments need more room, more supplies, etc. Rectors and Vestry members should expect facilities to be a big part of the leadership dynamic at this stage of growth. They are also managing greater levels of money and need appropriate accountability and controls.

Application

So, which one are you? Are you the home school model, the elementary grade school, the high school, or the college? It might even be less a function of size and more a function of culture and temperament of the leader (Rector) and board (Vestry). The kind of church you are will also have a lot to do with the culture around you, the size of the community where you live, and frankly, the kind of churches that are already in your community.

There is a telling way to find out what kind of school/church you are in. Think back last week to that part of the Sunday morning service that is standard to every church: The Announcements. What was said? Who said it? What did they talk about?

You know the drill. At some point in the service, before, middle, or after, someone tells everyone else what are the important things to know about the church as the week, months, or seasons roll on. Imagine that "Announcement Moment" in each of these four churches.

The Home School Church

The leader of the service stands up at the time of the announcements and says, *"Good morning. I can see most of us made it today. I know its cold out-side, but thankfully, Betty has plugged in the coffee pot. It will be hot by the time we are through with our service."* There is a pause while the leader looks over some notes and then turns to one of the most tenured members and says, *"Bill, did you want to say anything about the upcoming parish meeting?"* Bill makes his announcement and then sits down. The priest then says, *"Okay, well, let's talk about who is in the hospital and who needs our prayers this week..."*

The Grade School Church

The Rector stands up and says, *"Good morning. I tried to greet you all as you came into church this morning, but if I didn't don't take it personally. I'll be at the back of the church to shake your hand on your way out."* There is a slight pause before he continues. *"I am starting a bible study for men this weekend and looking forward to it. We have had a few sign-ups, but we could use a few more men to come join us. We are having a Cornhole Tournament after the study."* There is another slight pause. *"Oh, one more thing, we are getting some youth coming here from time to time. If you have any experience in leading teen-agers, I need your help with that. I am totally committed to reaching the youth of our community. If you can help or know someone who can, please talk to Linda after the service."* Linda is his wife and the mother of their two teenagers.

The High School Church

The Rector or the Associate Rector stands up in front of the congregation and says, *"Good morning. You can read all about our programs and activities in your bulletin this morning and on the website. We have lots going on for the new people to join! But today, we have some great news about our upcoming mission trip. We are leaving in two weeks and I want you to meet Frank and Stacy Miller who have organized it. Frank is the coach for our Men's softball team and Stacy is on staff here part-time. They are organizing the whole thing. Please welcome them as they come up and tell us more about the trip ahead and how you can support it with prayer and finances."*

The College Church

The Executive Pastor stands in front of the church body and says, *"Good morning. I'm glad we have all of our programs and announcements in the booklet in your pews. Please take one home to keep on your kitchen table. Your entire family will find things going on in our church just for them. But today, I want to remind you that our Rector has a clear vision about our relationship to the wider community. We want to get to know them and serve them in any way that we can. This morning, we have invited the Chief of Police to come and share some of the things that are going on around us and the ways that our church can be involved through prayer, support, and service to help the men and women in blue. Let's welcome Chief Williams up to have a word with us."* The Chief comes forward in uniform to a resounding amount of applause.

Do you see the difference? The **Home School Size Church** is like, well, a home. Everyone knows everyone else and knows where they are and where they are not. The **Grade School Size Church** has one person who is the central hub of activity, knowledge, direction, and plans. Nothing happens until that Rector comes into the room. The **High School Size Church** is active. People are attracted to that church because of what they are doing; their bulletin on Sunday morning reads like a 'menu' of programs that people can choose from. There are people in that church who have to be introduced by first <u>and</u> last name. (Frank and Stacy Miller) The Rector is functioning like a coach by trying to get the best out of everyone…making sure that everyone is playing the right position on the team. The **College Size Church** is nearly a 'city' unto itself. It has a vision to be a force for good within the larger community. It tries to make every Sunday a moment that you would never want to miss. It functions as a *presence* in the community.

I hope the four vignettes have been a helpful way of seeing how a church operates within its own culture and size. There is a 'vibe', so to speak, in each size and culture. And it would be very awkward to mix vibes. Could a small Home School church ever invite the Chief of Police in uniform? Yes, but not likely. And it would be awkward to say the least. Could you imagine a staff leader in a College size church telling interested youth volunteers to talk to a person named Linda? Who is Linda?

Who is Busy?

One more way to tell what kind of church you have is to ask, "Who is busy?" That is, who is pouring out their life, heart, soul, and career to help the church be all that God has called it to be? Look at who is the busiest person or group in the church, and you will probably find the type of church your congregation is.

Let me explain. In a **Home School Church**, the entire small congregation is usually busy. In a **Grade School Church**, it is the pastor that is swamped with work, preparing multiple topics and exercises every time the class is in session. In the **High School Church**, it is the members who are busy (many of them are paid staff, albeit part-time). They are organized into activities and programs so that, as it seems to me, every person needs their key or door entry code! Finally, in the **College Church,** the entire staff and campus is always a busy hub of activities with events, speakers, symposiums, and exciting programs that draw from a wide spectrum of people.

Do you like this metaphor? There is another way it is helpful. Think about the role of the Rector in each of these categories. In the Home School Church, the Rector is a chaplain to the family. In the Grade School Church, the Rector's role is like a Father of the family. In the High School Church, the Rector is a Coach. And in the large College Size Church, the Rector is more like a Mayor.

Perhaps this chart will sum everything up. There is a lot to it. Where is your church in each of these categories?

	Who is Busy?	Visitors Are...	Why Visitors Come	Rector Is...	Vestry...
Home School	Everyone	Rare	Church Event	Chaplain	Does Everything
Elementary	Rector	Welcomed	Rector Recruits	Father	Helps the Rector
High School	Members	Enlisted	Members Invite	Coach	Gives Insight
College	Staff	Overseen	Programs	Mayor	Protects Values

Now that we have framed out the issues and the culture that size develops and determines, we can look at the specific roles of the Rector, Wardens, and the Vestry in the following chapters. Each role will have to find its expression within the culture of its specific church. But I hope you can see how important it is to find the right person for the right culture and size of a congregation.

VI. THE ROLE
OF THE RECTOR

THOSE WHO ARE NEW to the Anglican tradition will find a world of titles, positions, and names that might seem a bit foreign, if not antique. These are fair questions to ask: What is a Vicar? Does my church really need a Warden? Really? What is the difference between a Rector, a Senior Pastor, and a priest? In this section, I hope to offer the answers to these questions.

First, let's get some basic words defined. There are many new terms and titles to know, to be sure, but these are some of the basics ones you might need to know.

- **Rector**: The ordained priest who is the elected and/or appointed spiritual leader of a congregation. The title is nearly synonymous with "Senior Pastor."

- **Associate Rector**: This is an ordained priest who is responsible for a broad scope of programs and who also helps shape the vision and mission of the church.

- **Assistant**: This is an ordained deacon or priest

who is overseeing a specific area of ministry or program such as Youth Ministry, Christian Education, or Pastoral Care.

- **Parish**: In the ACNA, there is no standard definition of what a parish is, but it is usually a self-supporting congregation that is part of a wider collection of parishes called a Diocese.

- **Mission**: Again, there is no standard definition of a mission, but generally speaking it refers to a congregation that is small and not financially self-sufficient.

- **Vicar**: When the term is used for a congregational leader, a "vicar" is one who stands in the place (vicarious) for the Bishop. He/she is the Bishop's appointee and the Vestry is thus the Bishop's to control and oversee. In some dioceses the Vestry of a Mission is not called "Vestry" but "Bishop's Committee." The Vicar functions as a fully ordained priest but usually, because of size or youth, the congregation is not able to support itself.

- **Canon**: A Canon can be one of these two things or both. A Canon is either an assisting priest on a cathedral or Bishop's staff, or a recognized leader whose ministry, in effect, sets a standard of excellence. Lay people can be Canons. Only a Bishop can appoint a Canon. Also, if a Canon is made by a Bishop as a "standard" or exemplary leader, that title will stay with him or her for life.

- **Dean**: A Dean can be one of two things, or both. A Dean can be the head of a cathedral in a diocese. This title of Dean is analogous to the title of Rector of a parish. But he can also be a minister who has jurisdictional authority or responsibility. Or he can be the head of a seminary or graduate school. The title does not stay with the person when they leave.

- **Wardens**: These are elected/appointed laypeople from the elected group of the Vestry. I have included a chapter in the book on the work of the wardens.

There is a high degree of variety on the use of these terms or roles, and they can vary according to local customs and history. For instance, I know of many small mission, non-self-sustaining churches where the congregational leader is a part-time priest and is referred to as a Rector. In the formation stage of the ACNA, this is to be expected.

For the purposes of this chapter, I am going to assume that a Rector is the leader of a self-sufficient parish in a diocese.

Every Parish needs to be led by a Rector. The Provincial Canons call for this fact. There must be a Rector,

Acting Rector, or a Priest in Charge for every congregation under a Bishop. However, in a unique "nod" to the local authority and autonomy of the congregations and diocese, the role of the Rector is not spelled out explicitly in the Canons of the national body. In fact, the canons state specifically that Rectors and clergy and the roles and duties they must assume are under their own Bishop and governance in their own diocese.

> *Norms for the calling, duties and support of Rectors and other Clergy, and the dissolution of a pastoral relation shall be provided by each Diocese. Rectors shall be domiciled in the diocese to which their congregation belongs.[1]*

The diocese, then, not the national body, plays a large role in determining the roles, responsibilities, and duties of the Rector in each diocese. There is usually a good deal of latitude given from the Bishops, and there are over two dozen different dioceses. Thus, it is impossible to spell out the specific roles and responsibilities of the Rector of a congregation. But the Canons of both the Province, which are scant, and the Canons of each diocese, determine the standards under which Rectors and other clergy function. No priest has *carte blanche* to lead their congregation however they want. Their Bishop is truly their overseer.

---

1 This quote is from the current version of the Constitutions and Canons of the Anglican Church in North America, pg. 25.

However, from a governance overview, we can say this much: The Vestry collaborates with the Rector in the temporal and spiritual leadership of the Congregation. It is also clear that the Rector has a unique level of autonomy under the direction of the Bishop—especially in the vision, worship, and program life of the parish. Also, the Rector is part of the governing board and serves as its Presiding Officer. This gives us canonical clarity, but what does it look like in practice?

"Rector" Is a Ministry

If we focus on the unique leadership and institutional role of the Rector, we learn the obvious: A Rector is a priest, or presbyter, in the Church. The Rector can be a Bishop as well. But the reverse is not necessarily true. All priests and Bishops are not Rectors. There are requirements and assumptions that pertain to all priests in the Church, and a Rector is surely expected to fulfill those requirements. The Ordinal in the 2019 Book of Common Prayer (2019) outlines the weighty calling of those called and commissioned as priests in God's Church.

- *Every priest is called "to teach, to warn, to feed, and to provide for the Lord's family, and to seek for Christ's sheep who are in the midst of this fallen world, that they may be saved through Christ forever."*

- *Every priest is given the task to "work diligently,*

with your whole heart, to bring those in your care into the unity of the faith and of the knowledge of God, and to maturity in Christ."

- *Every priest is commanded to "equip and lead your Congregation to proclaim tirelessly the Gospel of Jesus Christ." By the power of the Holy Spirit and with humility, each priest is called to care for God's people and commanded to "be a faithful minister of God's holy Word and Sacraments."*

- *Every priest is called to be "a wholesome example and pattern to the flock of Christ."*

This is the role and responsibilities for every person who is ordained as a priest in the church. Essentially, we all take the same vows during the ordination service.

But a Rector exercises a unique role as a priest in the church. It is at this point that a Vestry member should begin to see a difference between the functions and duties of a priest (which all priests shares) and the role and responsibilities of the Rector of a church.

The Five Roles of the Rector

I want to give an overview from my years of experience as a Rector and observing and working with congregations. I quickly add that my overview below is only my opinion. It does not have the weight of a Canon at all. But whatever wisdom I might share with you on this subject is born of experience and conversation with many other Rectors.

There are certain things that should be on the Rector's "job description" that are not on the job description of any other priest in the church. This means that the Rector needs to be willing to lead in areas that no other priest or Vestry leader can or should. The Rector cannot abdicate these five key areas.

1. Lead the Vision

The Rector's primary task as Rector is to articulate, preach, teach, interpret, uphold, exemplify, shape, and develop the stated purpose of the parish so that it becomes the focal point for the congregation. Most of the time, this purpose is contained in some kind of mission or vision statement. But regardless of how it is stated or encapsulated, the Rector has this very unique role as principle spokesman. This is what visionary leadership means.

It isn't enough to come up with a great vision or an exciting idea about the future. The Rector must become adept at leading *toward* a vision that is biblical and Gospel-centered. When the Rector leads toward a vision, he or she will continually explain and expound how God has (in ages past), is now currently, using his people for the work of the Gospel.

Here is another way to say it: The Rector should be laboring to point the people toward the vision or mission of the church. Much of the work of the Rector is simply this: to remind, remember, reflect, and rehash the direction of the congregation.

This is a very handy way to think about this aspect of the Rector's role. The way a Rector can lead toward the vision is to actively and consistently point the people toward a common vision. It is a very good idea to examine every program with the parish with this question in mind: *Does this program, activity, expenditure, effort, service, staff position, function, task, meeting, group, event, new building, or developmental work point the people of the parish toward the mission of our congregation?*

2. Build the Team

The Rector should not be a Lone Ranger. When the vision is clearly articulated, the Rector has the obligation to build a team of people who can help move the church in the fulfillment of that purpose. There are groups and committees and staff, whether paid or volunteers, who need the voice and the touch of the Rector on a routine basis. However, the Vestry is just one of the groups that are servant leaders who help the vision of the parish become a reality.

As Anglicans, we value clean lines and godly order. Here the line is clean and clear. *The Rector oversees the team.* Oversight of the teams or ministries is not the role of the Vestry or any liaison from the Vestry. This is an important distinction because often the Rector sees the Vestry as adjunct staff or liaison committee leaders. The Rector can make that assignment if desired, but the point remains the same. It is the Rector that oversees the committee or the group.

This is what is meant by the Latin phrase, *ex officio*, or "from the office" of the Rector. The Rector is an *ex officio* member of every guild, group, committee, task force, or team in the parish. This means that, by virtue of the office of Rector, the Rector is on every team, guild, or group regardless of whether he or she is present for the meeting.

It is important to note that the Rector should not be required, or even expected, to attend every meeting of every committee, chapter, program, function, or guild in the congregation. The purpose of this by-law or canon (it is usually a canon of the diocese) is to ensure that the Rector has complete control over the program and processes that make a church work. If I put this privilege another way, it might sound a bit more pointed: "The Rector is always welcome to attend, participate, direct, or disband any group within the parish."

There is usually flexibility in the dynamic of this reality based on church size (which we will talk about in another section of this book), but the point holds that the Rector gives oversight and management.

3. Provide for the People

The Rector has a unique leadership role in the area of shepherding. He or she is to provide for the people. There are many things the people need (some of them they even want!) that the Rector should make sure they receive: pastoral care, meaningful worship, gospel-centered programs, sound teaching, clear communication, sound administration, marriage preparation, community engagement, outreach ministry, deployment in mission, prayerful counsel, and so much more. The Rector doesn't do all of these things, but the Rector provides by making sure that these are provided for in the parish.

I want to be a bit clearer about this role as "provider." Many in the Anglican tradition refer to a priest as "Father" or abbreviated "Fr." This is very common. It comes from the long-standing idea of the priest as a spiritual father of the faith for many people. Indeed, as a priest, we often feel as though we are a spiritual parent to many believers, as the Apostle Paul was a spiritual father to the young Timothy. But while all priests can be a spiritual parent to people in the parish, the role and ministry of a Rector is not to be the Father of the congregation. Rectors who assume that they are the Father of the church family invite all kinds of personal needs and emotional crosscurrents in the church to be projected onto themselves. Not only is this a dangerous dynamic, it is also an impossible task. God is the Father, Jesus Christ is the head pastor/shepherd, and the Holy Spirit is the welcomed power to do the work.

In other words, the title and role of "Father" could be applied to the office of the priest, but, in my opinion, not to the role of Rector.

To provide for the people, as we have seen above, a more apt title for the Rector might be that of coach or mayor. His or her role is to ensure that the people are cared for and attended to authentically and appropriately. The Rector should ask, "What do these people of God need to grow more committed to the Lord and His Gospel and more sensitive and obedient to the leading of the Holy Spirit?"

What whatever the answer is to that question, the Rector seeks to provide.

4. Maintain Accountability

There is another reason why the role of "Father" should only apply to the priestly office and not to the role of Rector. The Rector and all priests and deacons are not members of the congregation they serve. Very few people know this, but it is canonically accurate. The priests and Rector are members of the Diocese where they are canonically resident. They are held accountable by the Bishop for the health and strength of the church they serve and of their own personal and spiritual life.

Most Vestries and certainly most people in their congregations do not know that their Rector is not a member of their congregation. Neither are any of the ordained leaders. This makes the point above even more explicit. The priest may be a Rector, and he may be called "Father" out of a sense of respect and tradition. And he may be a spiritual father to many people in the congregation. But he is not the father of the congregation.

With this said, it is important that the Rector determine how and when to be accountable to someone. This 'accountability' goes far beyond submitting to an annual evaluation. (We will cover this in the Appendix.) Accountability for the Rector means that he or she willing place themselves in a position of humility relative to other spiritual and peer leaders. What does this look like? For some, it will be a routine appointment with a spiritual director. For others, it could be an annual retreat, personal or marriage counseling, Sabbath-taking disciplines, peer group learning communities, and other efforts to protect and preserve an inner life with God. This is a matter of the heart. It cannot be dictated, but it can be encouraged by the members of the Vestry and monitored by the Wardens or the bishop. Supporting the Rector in this area should be a funding priority by the Vestry.

What is at the heart of this issue of accountability is the very unique position that a Rector is in. It is a burden to carry the spiritual weight of an entire church. But it is also a blessing. Each Rector must have the personal self-awareness to know when to set the burden down and get rest, perspective, and refreshment.

5. Develop Stewardship

The Rector has a huge responsibility for the stewardship of everything in and of the parish. Of course, this means money, as we shall see. But it means so much more than money. To be a steward of the parish, in this sense, is to be a custodian of the people, property, and opportunity that the congregation has for the furtherance of the Gospel. The Rector is responsible for how the parish is fully aware of the mission it is called to engage. This is a privilege for a priest to undertake as a Rector, but no one should doubt the gravity of the task or the weight of the responsibility.

If your Rector was formally installed as the Rector of the parish by the Bishop, chances are he or she prayed this prayer or one with similar intentions and sentiment. Read through this prayer[2] carefully.

> O Lord my God, I am not worthy to have you *come under my roof; yet you have called your servant to stand in your house, and to serve at your altar. To you and to your service I devote myself, body, soul, and spirit. Fill my memory with the record of your mighty works;*

2 This weighty prayer is taken from the Book of Common Prayer, 2019.

enlighten my understanding with the light of your Holy Spirit; and may all the desires of my heart and will center in what you would have me do. Make me an instrument of your salvation for the people entrusted to my care and grant that I may faithfully preach the Gospel and administer your holy Sacraments, and by my life and teaching set forth your true and living Word. Be always with me in carrying out the duties of my ministry. In prayer, quicken my devotion; in praises, heighten my love and gratitude; in preaching, give me readiness of thought and expression; in worship, increase my zeal for godly preparation; and grant that, by the clearness and brightness of your holy Word, all the world may be drawn into your blessed kingdom. All this I ask for the sake of your Son our Savior Jesus Christ. **Amen.**

It is easy to see why the Rector needs to have a steady life of prayer and why the Rector needs to be prayed for and prayed with regularly. This is a heavy load.

But an essential part of the load is to carry the responsibility and the burden of stewardship. He or she must function as the steward of everything under the care of the parish. This will undoubtedly mean developing members and families to be stewards of their personal financial resources as well as their abilities, temperament, and time.

But it will also mean that the Rector is in charge of raising the money to supply the resources for the congregation. He or she must have a biblically developed confidence to raise the financial resources needed while simultaneously providing the congregation with the discipleship opportunity of growing in generosity. The Vestry can help in this area, but they are not the primary fundraisers. The buck stops, or rather starts, with the Rector. Helping the congregation understand the biblical use of money, articulating a theology of stewardship, and challenging people to give is one of the most rewarding and impactful things a Rector can do, and only the Rector can do it.

Hence the need for constant prayer by and for the Rector.

The Rector Is a Truck Driver

I find it helpful to think about the unique role of the Rector with a visual illustration. I bought my first truck several years ago—a Toyota Tacoma. We call those "Tacos" for short here in Texas! Driving around in that truck has helped to give me a picture of what it means to be a Rector. It's a picture that other Rectors, Vestries, and congregations can all understand.

Like any driver, the Rector needs to see clearly! The Rector's role is to look through the "windshield" and declare which road is to be taken. Vision is always about direction to a distant horizon. Where are we going? The Rector's role should be very vocal and clear: This is the place where we are headed. This is what I can see through the windshield. Think of Moses and the task he had leading people on the path directly ahead. He doesn't just say we are going to the Promised Land—he paints the picture of the Promised Land and what it would be like for the people to live there.

For example, in Deuteronomy 8:7–10 Moses fulfills the Rector's role perfectly. He says,

> *For the Lord your God is bringing you into a good land, a land of brooks of water, of fountains and springs, flowing out in the valleys and hills, a land of wheat and barley, of vines and fig trees and pomegranates, a land of olive trees and honey, a land in which you will eat bread without scarcity, in which you will lack nothing, a land whose stones are iron, and out of whose hills you can dig copper. And you shall eat and be full, and you shall bless the Lord your God for the good land he has given you.*

Look at the level of detail. Moses describes not only where they are going (the Promised Land) but what it will be like when they get there. He describes the ease and joy that they will experience. He answers the unspoken question that everyone asks of their leader one way or the other, "What's in this for me and my family?"

The Rector looks through the windshield toward the horizon and tells everyone about where they are going and what it will be like when they get there. And as Moses attributed both the journey and the destination to God, so too, the Rector should help people remember who to bless and thank for it all. Not to mention who owns the truck!

Of course, drivers also check the mirrors and are aware of their surroundings and the road traveled. Rectors do this too. While looking through the windshield charting the path ahead, the Rector looks in the rear-view mirrors to help the church understand and interpret their past. Again, only the Rector can do this.

The Rector needs to be honest about the past and help the church know what can be learned, celebrated, or grieved from the past to keep driving forward. Telling the church's story can't just be a triumphant catalogue of success that glosses over failures or whitewashes painful experiences. The Rector should help everyone ask and answer: *What was God doing then? Where was He telling us to go? How has the Lord guided and directed us?*

Is it too much to stretch the analogy a bit here? For example, most automobiles have three different ways of looking behind them. A single viewpoint will not do. There are blind spots in the past that certain people cannot see; it is not in their field of view. It is important to see the past clearly and soberly.

But it is also true that the mirrors looking to the past are *smaller by far* than the windshield. The future for a church is broad and bright when its Rector focuses time, prayer, energy, and passion on what is ahead. The future is dim and boring if the Rector keeps looking into the past trying to retrieve or relive what has already happened. By some actual measurements, the future-facing windshield is 80 to 100 times larger than the rear-view mirror. This alone tells us where we should be focusing our time and attention. Forward!

Finally, trucks have truck beds. They can haul things, unlike other automobiles. I mentioned earlier that the Rector has a ministry of provision. Think about it like a truck bed. The Rector must figure out what to pack and haul for the journey. The Rector must determine what cargo space is available and bring the right stuff, programs, and emphases for where the church is headed. A friend of mine once said, "David, you can do anything you want, but you can't do everything you want." That short pithy statement is so clear and true it should be placed on a bumper sticker on the truck! A church can't do everything. There is limited cargo space. A pickup truck can carry only the essentials. Thus, the Rector leads the way in figuring out what to pack and what can't be taken along on the journey.

The Rector drives the truck.

When I think about the role of the Rector in the life of the church, I want to add an obvious but important point. *There is only one Rector.* And, to make the point even more clearly, <u>there can be only one Rector</u>. There will always be people riding shotgun, as we used to say in Arizona. There will be people in the backseat. There might even be folks under the hood, as it were. But there is and should only be one Rector.

A church should pray for wise and committed leaders on the Vestry. They are needed to help, advise, consent, support, pray, develop, and give vital perspectives and wisdom. There can be multiple priests and deacons and even Bishops that reside on staff or work in the parish ministry. There can be other ordained leaders that preach sermons from time to time and lead worship regularly. But there is only one Rector.

Rector as Ruler?
In my effort to make the case for this important role of the Rector, I want to quickly add that the Rector is not a ruler; he should never be bullheaded, stubborn, or an autocrat. Every Rector needs good and wise counsel who will be honest and forthright with

him. He or she needs to keep in mind that the sacred charge of leadership is a gift that can be easily abused or handled in a rough manner.

The Rector does not need a chorus of nay-sayers or yea-sayers. He needs honest and godly people who will tell the truth about the impact and effect of any likely decisions *before* they are made. The Rector needs to listen to this counsel and, when he hears enough pushback from trusted leaders, delay, postpone, or rethink.

A Rector should never spring new, great, big ideas on the Vestry and expect members to ratify them in one meeting. The Rector should probably never use "Surprise" as a strategy for ministry. Each new idea cannot be rammed through or pushed on to the Vestry. There always needs to be a time of discussion, discernment, prayer, and finally, decision. The Rector needs to be quick about things slowly. Let people hear the idea, ask relevant questions, discern together, offer suggestions and adaptations, and take time for godly counsel. People need to test the ideas of the leader, no matter how good the ideas are or how gifted the leader is.

One of the greatest maxims I ever heard has saved me countless hours of meetings and personal heartaches. I was told years ago that people love change…but they do not like to be changed. Wise words. It is an axiomatic truth that elected boards of volunteer leaders take their tasks seriously, and they want to take needed time to think, pray, and gain discernment.

Still, only the Rector can do the three things that are necessary: point to the future vision, interpret the past, and provide for the journey. And only the Rector *should* do these three things. *If the Rector does not do these things, the church will not move.* And if anyone else, including the Vestry or anyone on the Vestry, does any of these three things instead of the Rector, there will be conflict and strife. This is precisely why, according to most parish by-laws, the Vestry is not to meet together without the expressed consent of its Rector.

Gifting and Growing

In outlining the roles of the Rector and the roles (next) of the Wardens and Vestry, I think often of a teeter-totter going up and down. There is a give and take relationship between Rector and Vestry that, when it is moving and active, is a beautiful thing to see. On the one hand, the Rector has tenure; the Rector is in charge of the entire staff; the Rector has the sole responsibility to provide the worship and educational program for the entire congregation. He should be a man of prayer and know how the Lord would have him lead. He should be clear and authoritative. But he should know not to be authoritarian. The Vestry members are elected members of the church who want to put their gifts in service of the Lord and his church. They are not a rubber-stamping group.

Also, we know that the Wardens and Vestry needs to be supportive of the Rector; he is the one in charge. But they should have prayerful input and their personal leadership honored and encouraged.

As I consult the parishes that are dwindling in numbers, energy, and mission, one of the most common things I see is this teeter-totter *stuck* in one position. Either the Rector is too timid, doesn't know what to do, and constantly looks to the Vestry for encouragement and suggestions. Or the Vestry is over-controlling and wants to vote on everything that is proposed as a program; they want to approve every expenditure. Or vice-versa: The Rector is bullish on his or her own ideas and pushes them on to the Vestry and the parish. Or the Vestry is an uncommitted group of people who are just hoping that the Rector can pull a rabbit out of a hat!

It is a question of gifting and leadership. Some leaders lead by consensus; some leaders lead by encouragement; some lead by inspiration. On the Vestry, and within the Vestry retreats, discussion, and sidebar conversations, the Vestry and Rector should be working together. Affirming each other's gifts and insights; prayerfully asking the Lord to lead the Rector, the Vestry, and the Church together. In other words, there is to be a dynamic balance between the two.

VI. THE ROLE OF THE RECTOR

Indeed, the Vestry does have a vital role in helping the Rector see the future, interpret the past, and provide for the journey as suggested above. They are his/her sounding board, advisors, supporters, challengers, truth-tellers, advocates and prayer partners. In the next chapter, I will outline the invaluable roles of the Wardens. And in the following chapter, I will turn to the important responsibility of the Vestry.

VII. THE WORK OF THE WARDENS

MY LAST SUMMER AT CHRIST CHURCH where I was Rector was a time of saying goodbye to many wonderful friends and co-laborers from the past 31 years of ministry. I am sure that you can imagine how emotional and wonderful it was to spend time over coffees, dinners, conversations, and after-church events thanking people for their love and support. My resignation as Rector was a surprise to most people, including me. I had imagined that I would have stayed in that role another 10 years. I truly had thought that. But when I turned 60 years old, I had a profound impression from God that I was to step aside and let a younger leader be called as Rector. I was sad to leave this great church, but I was confident that the Lord had given me this clear direction.

It took nearly a year for the search process to identify a candidate, issue a call, and then allow the slow wheels of our US Immigration Service to allow the next Rector to move to Plano and take over. When he moved to Plano to begin his role as Rector, I finished my rounds, cleaned out my office, and prepared to say goodbye at a public service in early August.

There was one last dinner I wanted to host. I wanted to honor and thank all the Sr. Wardens that had served at Christ Church over the years. I made a list of everyone who had served in that capacity and invited them to my home for supper. Unlike the meetings they had attended in their tenure as Sr. Warden, there would be no minutes, no formal reports, no financial reviews, and no votes cast. I only had one item on the agenda: thanksgiving.

There were 32 men and women who had stood with me for over three decades of work and ministry at Christ Church. One of the former wardens, Matt, had died a few years previously. One had moved away. Another warden and I had had a falling out and he graciously chose not to attend. One of the wardens from the past had joined a Roman Catholic church and, after his wife died, had become a Roman Catholic priest. One had joined another denomination. But that night, 27 wardens came to my home for my last Vestry meeting, as unofficial as it was.

Remembering God's Faithfulness

I had nothing but thanks to express to these friends. And they were all friends. They had been part of a story of growth and challenge during my time at Christ Church. We all shared memories of some hard-won accomplishments and some deeply felt losses. I had prepared only one question to ask the group that gathered together in my living room after dinner.

Emotion caught in my throat as I called the meeting to order. I thanked them all for coming. I expressed what it had meant to me to lead this church for so many years. And then I asked them the question I had prepared: "What do you remember of God's faithfulness in your time as a Senior Warden?"

The stories began. Some of the early wardens remembered the financial thin ice we used to skate on every year waiting for December (and the Lord) to make us whole. A few recounted the time when we "sent off" one of our many new church plants to a nearby community. Some told stories of personal growth as they learned to pray through some of the large vision-correction moments we faced. They all had prayed with me through the many years we wrestled with our denominational struggles in the Episcopal Church. Most everyone in the room remembered a building project. In fact, if you were a Sr. Warden at Christ Church, chances were very good that you had been part of one of our seven back-to-back 3-year capital campaigns to either build a building or pay off a debt.

If we had had the entire evening, we would have remembered the land purchases we negotiated, the architects and builders we interviewed and hired, the policies we had to enact as we expanded our campus, the architect we fired, the personnel issues we struggled with, the search processes we endured, the missionaries and Bishops we hosted, the field trips we took, and endless coffees we drank, plans we made, prayers we prayed, and fears we shared.

My leadership of the Vestry during those three decades was not without trials and hardships. But they were glad to be there. And I was glad that every one of them had come.

Wingman

The wardens were my wingmen, one by one, year by year. They were the ones that I knew I could call when I shouldn't call anyone else. Each warden had my back. If we disagreed in private meetings, we always agreed in public. There were a few times that my wardens "covered" for me when I made errors in judgement.

I remember once when I had to terminate a youth worker. It got ugly. The parents demanded a meeting. They wanted to know why. There was sufficient cause for the termination of this youth leader, but I did not want to disclose any details. I did not want to trigger a lawsuit. I just stood before the group of parents and hurt teenagers and asked them to trust my judgement. There was some murmuring and vocalizing, but I stood my ground. Just before it turned worse, the Sr. Warden stood up and walked to the front of the room and joined me at my side. He took the microphone and spoke to the room. He said that he knew the situation and that I had made the right decision. The murmuring ended and the meeting dispersed. He had my back.

In the early days of my ministry, a wise priest told me to never talk to the Vestry about my salary or any aspect of my personal compensation. I never did. Not once. But the wardens did. Most every year in the fall, they would come to me and ask how I was doing from a financial perspective. I would be frank with them. If it was tight for us, I would tell them. If we were doing okay, I would tell them. As the budget was presented at one of the last meetings of every year, the wardens would ask me to leave the meeting room and go home. They would talk about my own compensation and determine what increase, if any, I would receive.

The tradition in the Episcopal Church (where I came from) was to have two wardens, one called Junior and the other called Senior. In some churches the Rector selects the Sr. Warden and the Vestry selects the Jr. Warden. Sometimes this is a matter of tradition and/or by-law.

I worked a slightly different situation. I appointed the Sr. Warden and I asked the Vestry to elect a Jr. Warden. I met with them together month by month to review and prepare for Vestry meetings and to discuss other issues and challenges. When the Sr. Warden would rotate off the Vestry, I would appoint the Jr. Warden to that role, and the Vestry would elect another Jr. Warden. In this way, the Vestry would have some hand in the selection of the Sr. Warden by electing the Jr. Warden. I will be honest and admit that I routinely nominated a person to serve as Jr. Warden, knowing that he would be Sr. Warden soon.

All of my Sr. Wardens had been Jr. Wardens before.

My Wardens and I formed a three-person partnership year by year. We were an executive committee. They were my lay partners; they helped me see the world of the church through the eyes of people in the pews. And every one of my Sr. Wardens had been a Jr. Warden the year before.

What Wardens Do

We can all agree that the term "Warden" is an odd name. The church is not a prison and the Rector is not an inmate! But the term dates from the 14th century when a non-clerical (lay) person was appointed in every parish in England to be the intermediary between the Rector and the parish. The term is unique to Anglican polity.

The role of Warden is not tightly prescribed by the Canons of the church. Most congregations and Rector develop their own ideas about the role in a particular congregation. It is probable that the role will ebb and flow to fit the personality of the congregation, the Rector, and the size of the church.

It is impossible to outline the specific roles and responsibilities of the Sr. and Jr. Warden because they will vary so much according to tradition, size, and time availability of the lay person. But it should be known by all Vestries and certainly Sr. Wardens, that the role of the wardens is not an honorary title. It is a working title. It is a serious and very important role on the Vestry.

How serious? If the Rector's position is for any reason vacated or absented, the Sr. Warden is the one that will lead the church. The role does not fall to the assisting priest or the older staff member. The Sr. Warden is put in charge of the congregation. He or she is responsible for keeping the doors of the church open for public worship, appointing or leading a search process to find, elect, and call a new Rector, and for maintaining the financial obligations of the parish.

Three Questions
Every Senior Warden
Should Ask

As we will see, the Senior Warden is a role of significant responsibility and influence. The decision to choose who will serve as Senior Warden is usually left to the Rector. And it should be remembered that the role is not an honorary role. There is work to be done and, in the case of a vacancy of the office of Rector, a whole lot of work to be done.

A newly recruited Senior Warden might feel flattered or honored to be asked to serve the church in this way. That is a good sense to have, but I would advise that each candidate or nominee for Senior Warden prayerfully and thoughtfully answer these three questions in succession.

1. Do I believe in the stated and directional mission of this congregation?

2. Do I believe in the call and character of the Rector to lead this congregation at this point?

3. Would I want to go on vacation or 'hang out' with this Rector?

This first two questions have to do with the clarity of the vision and the character of the leader. But the third question is one of 'chemistry'. Is there a friendship and appreciation for this person (Rector) such that I would actually want to spend time and invest in an ongoing relationship?

VIII. THE ROLE
OF THE VESTRY

EARLIER, WE LAID OUT the Canonical framework for thinking about the Vestry:

There shall be a governing board of each congregation, often known as the vestry, which is chosen and serves according to applicable laws, diocesan canons, and the congregational by-laws. The Presbyter in charge of the congregation shall always be a member of the governing board and its presiding officer except as provided by diocesan canon. The governing board is responsible for the temporalities of the congregation and, except where otherwise provided by canon, supports the clergy in the spiritual leadership of the congregation.

It is key to point out that the members of the Vestry are elected by members of the congregation to work with the Rector to attend to the temporal (financial and practical) needs of the congregation and offer support in the spiritual leadership of the congregation. Generally, Vestry members serve three-year, staggered terms and are elected at the annual business meeting of the parish (which is often held in

January). They are required to be active members and to affirm the faith of the Church. Vestry membership is not (should not be) a popularity contest. The Church should look to spiritually mature leaders with gifts suitable to the duties of the Vestry.

I want to begin with some negative propositions. Many of our parishioners and clergy have either no history and experience of vestries or largely dysfunctional history and experience of vestries. Here are some things the Vestry is **_not_**.

An Elder Board
Many people are familiar with a model of church governance where qualified spiritual leaders are appointed to lead and pastor the congregation. Usually this is a non-rotating leadership position. While we want spiritually mature leaders on the Vestry for sure, our system is not an "appointment for life" model. The Rector is the one who has tenure, not members of the Vestry.

A Board of Deacons
In many congregational types of church governance, the deacon board does a lot of the practical work of the church. The deacons are not "Deacons" in the Anglican "ordained" sense. No Bishop has been involved in their ordination. They are, instead, the serving arm of the church. In our polity, the Vestry does serve the church, but they aren't simply a workforce.

Adjunct Staff

In some churches, Vestry members assume that they are to "do" the work of church by running programs or teaching courses. Sometimes a Vestry member can be assigned to be the point of contact with a particular program. It may work well to have different Vestry members support specific ministries, but this system falls short of ideal if for only one reason: The Vestry is a rotating group of people coming on and going off the Vestry every three years.

And of course, the Vestry are elected to their position irrespective of whatever gifts they have; staff are called to their role according to their gifts and abilities. In other words, it is not a foregone conclusion that every Vestry person will have the gifts needed to also serve in a staff role.

Group Representatives

Vestry members are not representatives of a particular constituency. They should not be nominated or elected because they are from the Youth Group, the Altar Guild, or have an allegiance to a particular style of worship or service time. They should not advocate for one group or another. Their deliberation and consideration must take in the whole of the congregation.

So, what is unique about the Vestry? What does the Vestry do that only the Vestry is called to do? Before I list the areas of oversight and details that the

Vestry must oversee, I want to list five roles that the Vestry has in the life of the congregation. As I mentioned above with regard to the Role of the Rector, I do not have a canonical warrant for all of these per se. That is, I cannot point to a specific Canon or by-law that dictates these five roles. But I can say with certainty that these five areas MUST be attended to.

1. Protect the Vision

The Vestry's primary role, in my experience, is to protect the stated vision of the church. Each Vestry member should know the overall goals and visionary direction of the congregation. The vision of a congregation is like a North Star. It is a fixed point of reference that is "out there." It is something that helps the entire congregation orient their efforts and develop their program with respect to this vision.

The vision of a church should not really change over time. It might be forgotten over a period of instability or vacant leadership, but a church should not be adopting a new idea for a vision every few years. If the Rector is newly elected, or if the church has transitioned to a new location or merged with another congregation, then remembering and recalibrating around a vision is a good thing.

In an Anglican church, the Vestry leadership rotates every year. It is usually against the Diocesan Canons to serve more than two consecutive three-year terms. Thus, there will always be change in the Vestry. New members will be elected each year, while other veterans will complete their term of service. Added to this change, there is an occasional transition of a Rector. All of this turnover presents a challenge to the congregation; they can actually forget who they are and what they are trying to accomplish.

This challenge is all the more reason why a Vestry should know and follow a clear vision year by year, season after season.

2. Support Methods and Means

Alongside protecting the vision of a congregation, the Vestry should help the Rector develop effective methods or means to fulfill the vision. These are the plans, resources, and programs by which the congregation pursues the vision. If, as was mentioned, the vision is like a North Star and sets the direction of the church, methods and means are how the church moves forward. In the world of business, the methods of a church would be akin to the strategic plans that a company might have. Methods and means of a church usually do not change quickly or easily, but they need to be evaluated on a routine basis.

Let's look at an example. One church I consulted with worked, prayed, and, after some serious discernment and discussion, arrived at a clear vision of what God was calling their church to do. They were called to worship God, follow Christ, and go in mission to the outside world. This vision statement was based on multiple passages from Scripture, and their Vestry and staff truly owned it.

But when they were finished, they were concerned that the statement never articulated *how and what* they wanted to do. This is where the "methods and means" come in. These are the actual ways that a church actively decides to do, and then does. They began to make decisions and choices and arrived at four main actions they would pursue. They would focus and build their Worship Attendance, Small Group Discipleship, Neighborhood Evangelism, and Overseas Mission to a specific area of the world. These were four distinctive methods by which they were going to pursue their vision.[1]

Let me cite a negative example from my experience over the last few years. I worked with a medium-sized congregation a few years ago that proudly boasted that they had over 18 programs where members and visitors could "turn their faith into action." It sounded exciting to their Vestry, and they were busy trying to fund it all and keep every position active with volunteers. They were extremely committed to their vision, but their methodology lacked discernment or prayerful decision-making. Rather than focusing on only a few "methods and means," they boasted that they were dedicated to the mission of Christ "by all

1. In this discussion of vision, I hope you can see that a congregation never fully realizes their vision. A vision is a motivational direction that will carry the church in a faithful direction year after year. It is the desire for God that actually propels us to pursue Him. And, in this life, we never really arrive. In the next life, we do not have to go toward Him any longer. We are there!

means possible." I remember one meeting when I helped them count up the volunteers necessary to lead all the programs and, during the debriefing, several members of the Vestry realized that they were actually in charge of multiple programs. And they also realized that many people in the church were overly involved in multiple programs and even more members of the church were not involved at all. They activity was a 'false positive'.

They cut their programming by 60%, focused on only a few vital choices and a year later, the church grew.

A Rector and Vestry need to constantly ask this question: We say we have this vision, so, what are the methods and means by which we are pursuing it? Are the few programs that we have adequately staffed and funded? Are we expecting to have results from these means and methods?

This is one reason the Vestry must guard against getting swamped in the day to day operations of the parish and details of running the church. If they lose the bigger picture of the purpose and goals, they will not have the perspective to help the Rector see the mission field clearly.

The Vestry members work to build up, maintain, and ensure the means and methods are in alignment to pursue the vision. Mission clarity and well-funded means are key areas of Vestry leadership.

3. Uphold the Financial Integrity of the Church

One of the non-negotiable roles of the Vestry is to protect the financial integrity of the church. Through a designated finance team (and appointed Treasurer to lead that team), the Vestry should scrutinize the finances on a monthly basis. They should provide for an annual accounting of all funds and work with the Rector in developing the annual budget. They should be active in approving any long-term financial contracts or capital investments. They are fiduciary guardians of the financial life of the congregation to ensure that the church has a long-term future and is operating in a trustworthy way with all funds that have been generously given or responsibly borrowed.

This Canon (I.9, Sec. 3) from the Province spells out the duties this way.

> Financial responsibility and accountability are the obligations of the Church at every level… Every Diocese shall provide standards for record-keeping, financial accountability, insurance, investments and the bonding of financial officers for both the Diocese *and its congregations and missions.* (emphasis added)

The Vestry should be aware of what these standards are and how they are spelled out in the Canons for the diocese so that they can conform their practices at a minimum to those of the diocese. We will address these issues more later in the book.

4. Support the Rector as Spiritual Leader

The Rector leads the way for the congregation in vision, values, and the financial life of the church. The Vestry helps the Rector and supports this work. There is a delicate, working balance. The Vestry should never simply rubber stamp what the Rector advocates (especially in terms of the temporal matters of the church). They should represent the parish and the best interests of all the parish. This means that they should not be "devil's advocates" or a counterbalance for the Rector. As mentioned above, they should not have a constituency. They shouldn't narrowly represent a special interest group or specific program in the church. They should support the Rector and help wisely and prayerfully lead the vision, values, and finances.

This is not as easy as it sounds. People are very passionate about their faith and about their church. We would all hope they would be. And the Vestry's role should include being a clear sounding board for the Rector and learning to give honest feedback. But, at the end of the day, a Vestry cannot be divided on important issues, at least for long. And divisions or differences of opinion must be worked out and/ or ameliorated by wise counsel and clear teaching. If there is sustained conflict between the Vestry and the Rector, the Bishop's guidance and/or intervention may be needed.

Conflict is not uncommon in the church. We know this from the first pages of the Early Church in the Book of Acts. I cannot address this issue fully here. I honestly do not feel qualified, and there are many in our Anglican Church who are. But I want to make an important point about one kind of conflict: theological.

A Vestry is not a theological body; they are not set up for theological deliberation. Certainly, most of the members who are serving on a Vestry are not qualified to argue a theological or biblical point of view. These kinds of discussion are common in more "elder led" congregational churches, but the Anglican hierarchical church governance structure is not suited for it.

This does not mean there cannot be biblical teaching, spirited discussion, and theological debate. But in the Anglican system, the Vestry is suited for governance, not theology. If there is a need to settle a theological dispute or solve a biblical issue, both the Vestry and the Rector should invite the Bishop to attend their meeting, mediate the concern, and, if needed, render his opinion. It should be noted that if the Bishop renders his opinion in a formal sense (written) the matter should be considered settled.

The Vestry is elected to support the Rector and not to change his or her theology. This doesn't mean that there has to be 100% agreement about key ecclesiastical issues (such as, for example, the ordination of women to the priesthood or the meaning of the Holy Eucharist), but it does mean that the Vestry forum is not the place to settle these issues.

5. Model a Strong Commitment to Generosity

The final task of each Vestry member is to model sacrificial, tithe-based giving to the parish (along with the Rector, of course). The Vestry should be among the most generous and financially committed members of the church.

In my view, this may be the most important role of the Vestry, to model sacrificial giving. Why? I can quickly give four reasons why the Vestry should be made up of men and women who are committed to the tithe as the standard for giving in the local church.

- The Rector and Vestry will be challenging the congregation to generous, joyful, sacrificial giving. And it is a principle of leadership that one should not call people to go where the leaders cannot or do not go. As a matter of integrity, the Vestry cannot call the parish to sacrificial giving without being among those who give sacrificially too.

- A Vestry that is filled with committed and tithing people is going to be accustomed to the way God works with money and giving. They personally will be used to seeing God move miraculously in their own personal finances as they have given up for God. They will see it at the parish level too.

- On the reverse side of this, a Vestry that is not accustomed to seeing God move in their personal finances is usually very nervous about stepping out in faith. And, in all candor, that is all a church does! A church is usually walking by faith. The church budget is usually, at some level, a faith-walk all by itself. And if a church Vestry is nervous about expenditures or uncertain that God will really hear the prayers of His people, they will often be more concerned about conserving money than spending or investing it.

- Finally, a church Vestry should be committed to tithing because, frankly, there is more money to spend, give, or use for the Kingdom mission of God. Donors on the Vestry will excite donors in the congregation and the community. They will see how money can be used as muscle.

For these reasons, and a host of others, the Vestry should, one by one, have people on it that understand and model the high call of stewardship in their own life. They should be generous and open-handed with the resources that God has given to them. And they should be able to speak and lead as committed disciples of Christ at every level of their lives.

A generous culture will make the financial side of Vestry leadership much more fun and doable!

Money is muscle, a friend of mine would say. He could not have been more correct. A church with the right vision and the best values is not going to be able to do much if they do not have the financial strength to build their ministry.

But money is a powerful tool in the life of the church. It is useful to God for His work. It is an effective method of change in a community. But money must be managed and administered in the most effective and honorable way so that the work can be done with highest regard. Now we turn to the issues that are certain to be on the agenda of every Vestry meeting.

IX. FINANCIAL CONCERNS

EVERY VESTRY will be involved in the financial life of the congregation. Whatever size dynamics exist, the parish finances are one of the main things the Vestry gives attention to together. Remember, we want to be good stewards of the gifts that God entrusts to us through the generosity of His people. Everything done must be wise, careful, legal, and "above reproach."

Vestry members do not need to be professional bankers or accountants, but there needs to be a basic level of competence to lead in this area. It may be that the Vestry and/or the Rector needs some additional training in this area. Sloppiness (or worse, malfeasance) in the area of finances is like having a rotten trellis. It will eventually be disastrous for the congregation and there may be liability for the Rector and Vestry. This is an area for sound administrative leadership and processes.

One of the duties of the Vestry will be to appoint a treasurer. The treasurer will work with the designated finance committee and any staff members that serve in this key area. That does require a greater level of expertise in financial matters. Beyond that, there are at least two areas of finances that the Vestry must be attentive to for good health—financial protocols and financial oversight. This is not merely doing business as usual. It is part of the spiritual leadership of the parish. By the way, the Rector must be involved in this process too. They need to understand the basics of cash position, cash flow, fund-raising, and the trends of the church. The Rector gives leadership and works with the Vestry on financial issues.[1]

Provide Financial Oversight

Part of the agenda at each monthly Vestry meeting will be a financial report. And a part of the annual cycle of Vestry work will be the annual budget. At minimum each month, there should be two pieces of information. The first is a balance sheet reflecting the current cash position, assets, and liabilities of the parish. The second is a profit/loss statement (by account) for the previous month. These are vital to understanding the financial health of the parish and monitoring the finances. Some Vestry members will be more familiar with these reports than others. I would recommend that a basic orientation and refreshment of these concepts be given at least once a year when the Vestry receives new members. The Vestry is responsible for ongoing monitoring and annual oversight.

A key annual step for vestries is preparing an operating budget. The financial manual from one of our ACNA dioceses (ADOTS) says *"All vestries should*

1 I address issues about budgeting in the section on Best Practices.

have a realistic budget in place every year. A budget is a plan for the management of the church's resources." It is the task of the Vestry to adopt the annual budget, though it is likely presented to the congregation at the annual meeting. Here again is where church size and leadership dynamics are key. The annual budgeting process for a school-house-size congregation will be very straightforward. Larger churches will require a more complex budgeting process with more and more reliance on the church staff to put together the budget that the Vestry would subsequently review. (I address this subject in the last chapter of this book.)

By the way, Vestry members should be aware of one very unusual reality that is common among all churches. There are thirteen months in the year! Yes, you read that correctly. In terms of expenses, there are 12 months of the year. We all know that. But for church, in terms of income, there are 13 months in a year; and December is about 2 months.

This is unnerving for new Vestry members who might see their church going underwater month by month. Income doesn't meet expenses. But the fact is that every church usually receives money at a slower rate than it spends money. Many of the expenses for a church are constant and predictable throughout the year. They are evenly distributed. But money comes in very unevenly. Some months are "lighter" than others. The last month of the calendar year sees a significant increase in giving. Rectors and the Vestry must understand historical giving patterns and cash flow dynamics to avoid misunderstanding in this area.

Maintaining Trust

Every church must have sound financial protocols. How is money handled? Who handles it? Who writes checks? Who approves expenditures? The answers to these will look different from parish to parish, but the Vestry must know the answers for their local context. They have a fiduciary responsibility to ensure that money is handled properly. The financial protocols—especially the internal controls—should comply with parish by-laws, diocesan policies, and state guidelines. At minimum, you should know the basic chain of possession for how the offering is collected, counted, and deposited. Who has access to the church bank account? Who has viewing privileges for donor records? A basic rule of thumb is that one is never enough. There should always be multiple people involved in this process.

Most of these protocols are common sense and they should be developed and well-understood by the members of the Vestry. They are not personal. All protocols and methods are developed as a matter of good, sound business practices.

Nothing I have written or included here should be construed as legal or financial advice. However, I want to make three statements as I end this section:

First, it is probably true that everyone in your church wants your church to succeed. I think we have to assume that this is true in all churches. Every member will attend and support your church by choice. You are the best church they have found. They are committed to the full health and vitality of your congregation.

This thought should be at the forefront of any person who is called to serve on the Vestry. The members of your church want to be part of a congregation that makes a difference in the lives of its members and the surrounding community for the Lord.

I realize that we are all sinners in need of a Savior. And I realize that there are some people who want to serve on the Vestry to harm the church or "correct" the Rector or change the service times for their own personal convenience. However, I have always believed that in a church, most people, for the most part and most of the time, want to see their church thrive.

Second, the people who elect people to the Vestry give the Vestry a high level of trust. They not only want their church to succeed but trust the Vestry will help it to succeed.

This trust is the glue that binds people to the vision

of the church and to its leaders. When people in the pews are called upon to pray for the future of the church or to give for the future of the church, they must have a deep trust in their leadership. They must have a deep conviction that there are people serving on the Vestry who can be trusted.

If members do not trust their Rector or the leaders on the Vestry, a church will circle its wagons and stall out. The congregation may be asked to give for a high-minded purpose, but if the people do not trust the leadership, the congregation will not respond.

This trust in the leadership is so special and vital to the organization that it must be vigilantly maintained year by year. Trust is key to the movement of the mission of the church and if there is mistrust, or broken trust, the movement will stop.

Third, trust is a durable commodity between the Vestry/Rector and members *until it is not*. Trust can quickly evaporate. Many people reading this book have served an organization that has suffered through the malfeasance of a board or the fall of the leader due to misjudgments about money. Sadly, it is not uncommon. We have all heard of situations where financial misdealing is discovered.

These three statements should form the framework for a few "best practices" that the Vestry and ordained leadership should hold fast to. They may not all be doable right away, but at the very least, they should be seen as a goal for the church and its leadership.

Know the Financial Condition of the Church

1. The Vestry should have a financial audit of its books on a regular basis. I realize that a signed audit by a professional CPA is an expensive item to budget for. But there are ways of reducing the cost of an audit by scheduling it during an off season for a CPA firm or even performing it every other year. And did you know that there are "lesser" audits that can be performed by accounting firms? I am not an accountant by any means, but I know the Vestry should take a very careful look at the methods for handling cash and setting in place some serious safeguards. Sometimes a volunteer or retired CPA in the parish might perform an informal audit.

2. On a month to month basis, the Vestry should have an overview of the financial condition of the church. They do not need to have an in-depth analysis of the giving or spending trends in the church. Most financial reports should be limited to a single page and about 20 minutes. A treasurer or a warden can cover the high (or low) point in that amount of space and time. This does not mean that the Vestry would want to have only cursory reviews of the fi-

nancial life of the church. There should be some kind of review group or financial committee that can help review the accounts at a granular level. If the entire Vestry gets into the weeds on financial items, they will disappear into those details and lose the big picture. Again, the Vestry should review the parish finances, but they should be listed on a single page and the report should not take more than 20 minutes.

3. The Rector should maintain an arm's length approach to the financial reporting, counting, and distribution of funds. Therefore, he should never be the one to present the financial report to the Vestry. He or she should always be present to answer questions and/or give assurances. And his role in the parish should be to maintain a spiritual integrity even when it comes to the financial knowledge of what members give.

4. The Rector should never handle the offering at a worship service. This is an internal check to safeguard the Rector and the Vestry. Imagine that a new member of the church or a visitor sees that a priest of the church comes to the altar table at the end of a worship service and removes the offering plate, carrying it to an undisclosed location. Some other person such as an usher, altar guild member, or administrative assistant should be assigned this task.

5. The offering given during a worship service should be immediately placed in a lockable deposit bag and stored until the next opportunity for it to be counted and recorded. And, it goes without saying, the counting of the offering should never be done by only one person and never by the same two people week by week.

These safeguards would probably never be a necessity in your congregation. Most of the churches are close-knit collections of people who love and trust one another. But nevertheless, it is incumbent upon the Vestry to develop and maintain clear safeguards against any malfeasance or even the appearance of casual financial management.

Be advised: The price of following financial safeguards might not be free, but the cost of not doing so could be astronomical.

There are at least ten areas that the Vestry needs to oversee or provide oversight for.

1. Discretionary Funds

It is normal for the Rector to have funds that can be used at his/her discretion. By nature, these gifts are intended to be discreet and given under the exclusive discretion of the Rector. The Rector is often in a closer and more pastoral relationship with the people of the parish that allows him/her to see the true human needs that exist. Or, for example, a

Rector may know a seminarian that needs financial support. The Rector can decide to give a donation to a mission fund or a worthy faith-based project that supports or amplifies the vision of the church.

Typically, the needs that a Discretionary Fund is set up to meet are, as mentioned, discreet. These needs are, by nature, unbudgeted or under-funded. Sometimes they are brought to the attention of the Rector suddenly. In my view, a Vestry should set up a Rector's Discretionary Fund at the bank. It should be communicated to the members of the parish that this benevolence fund exists so that they can make donations to it. And the Rectors should be able to direct the use of this fund without general Vestry awareness.

However, you can immediately see the challenge that this might pose for the IRS or for an auditor. If the Rector has unbridled use over these funds, and they are fully hidden from the oversight of the Vestry, there will be many opportunities for misuse. And if these funds are misused, intentionally or innocently, this can short-circuit the level of trust in a congregation.

In my experience, the best safeguards for this kind of fund are as follows:

- A bookkeeper should keep records of the income and expenses for this fund. In other words, there should be no separate, hidden checking account or check book. This fund should be part of the church's restricted accounts.

- Members of the church can and should be invited to give to this fund in addition to the regular contributions they make.

- It is possible that a person would want to give money to the Rector's Discretionary Fund instead of the church's operating fund. This should be noted for the treasurer to see and account for in the financial records.

- The Rector should note the purpose of the expenditure on every check, and that description can be retrieved by the bookkeeper.

- Generally speaking, donors should not assume that they can direct the use of the money that they give to the Rector's Discretionary Fund.

- No funds from this account should ever be provided directly to the Rector or any member of his family.[2]

- The Rector should ask the Sr. Warden to review all expenditures on an annual basis. If there are two or three checks written for a regular or recurring need, the Warden should recommend that these expenses be covered by the Annual Budget of the church.

2 Thankfully I had wise leaders work with me in the early stages of the church I led. One area where I needed counsel was in the area of the Rector's Discretionary Fund. My nature is to NOT keep great records and be free and generous with the funds that were given. I am thankful that I took myself off the account as a signor and asked our finance staff to sign every check or have knowledge of every expenditure I made.

In the past, the IRS has had heartburn over the issue of the Rector's Discretionary Fund and some dioceses and Bishops strongly discourage it. The local Vestry should be sure they are aware of the challenges of a Discretionary Fund and provide the right safeguards. In some dioceses it is expressly forbidden by the Bishop for the church to have a Rector's Discretionary Fund. Local experience, history, and customs should be considered.

And, once again, it is always a good idea to ask someone on the Vestry or the Finance team to review the use of these funds on an annual basis. *While the use of the funds may be discreet, they are not to be confidential.*

2. Restricted and Designated Funds

In general, there are only two kinds of funds that come into a church. First, there are Unrestricted Funds that are freely given for the Operating Fund of the parish to pay salaries, bills, expenses, fund programs, and support the day to day operations of the church. The second kind of fund is a Restricted Fund. Some churches have many, many different kinds of Restricted Funds, but they are all treated the same.

In other words, there are only two kinds of funds: Unrestricted Funds that are given to operate and support the church. And everything else. There may be a Building Fund or a Flower Fund or a Vacation

Bible School Fund or a Mission Fund. But they are all the same kind of fund: restricted for use as designated by the Vestry.

Restricted Funds involve gifts to the church where either the donor(s) or the Vestry places restrictions on how the funds or assets may be spent or used. For example, if a donor restricts how a donation is to be used, the church has a legal, ethical, and moral obligation to use them as intended. If the church wants to use them for something else or in a slightly different manner, they need to talk with the donor about that to be clear and above reproach. There may be times where the church designates funds for a specific purpose. For example, they decide that the offering at a special service (like Ash Wednesday) be given to a local ministry partner. These kinds of things should be properly documented in the Vestry minutes and subject to the proper financial protocols.

It is not uncommon for older churches to have a plethora of unspent Restricted Funds in the bank. Again, they are all the same kind of money: Restricted. Believe it or not, some Vestries are paralyzed as to what to do with some of these funds. Perhaps the need for the funds' use has long since passed. The school that was being supported has closed its doors. The mission trip is over and funds that were collected and unused are sitting in the church's accounts.

This is not a serious problem for most Vestries, but funds should, after all, be used, re-directed, or returned to the donor. Here are a few bits of wisdom that I have picked up over the years.

- The Vestry can develop a simple policy to have a sunset on all Restricted Funds after a five-year period. That is, after a certain amount of time, the Vestry can reallocate Restricted Funds to a new purpose. This doesn't need to be trumpeted, but a standing policy will be a helpful tool.

- The Vestry can always refuse a donation. For example, if a donor gives a large gift that is directed to a pet cause or project that is not part of the church's mission, the Vestry can refuse or return the gift.

- Normally, a pastoral conversation between the Rector and the donor or the donor's family can free up a fund with stated but undesired restrictions.

Some Vestries like to have these unspent funds in their accounts for obvious reasons. It is a buffer or a cushion against a low balance in the Operating Fund. It is true. And while the funds in the Restricted Fund (of any variety) should not be permanently transferred to the Operating Fund, they can be "borrowed" during lean times. However, the presence of any large balances in the Restricted Fund can create some unintended consequences. First, they can create a false positive about the true financial condition of the church. The Vestry and members of the church might feel rather fortified by having a lot of money "on the side" and therefore might miss the warning signs of a church in stewardship trouble.

But there is at least one other reason why a high fund balance in the Restricted Fund might have some negative ramifications. The Vestry should remember that people give to a church for the congregation to use in the service of its mission. Funds are not supposed to be kept, hoarded, or stockpiled. Every church needs a "prudential reserve," but they do not need to be sitting on a lot of money. As donors see the "fattened" condition of the church's financial picture, they will give their money to another ministry or church.

3. Prudential Reserve

With regard to financial savings, a church Vestry will always need to have a full, prayerful, and honest conversation about the money it keeps in its "coffers" and the money it is spending for the mission and ministry.

Imagine your church receives a financial windfall. For some, this would be a major blessing. And for other churches, such a "blessing" would put them out of business. Why? Because they would not know what to do with that asset. Their members might cross their arms with satisfaction and thus close their wallets. People who had supported the church for years might feel their money was no longer needed. And the Vestry, now feeling flush with cash, might hire more staff than they need which would, in turn, turn off the volunteer strength of the church. It doesn't take too much imagination to think of how a huge windfall of money could cause a downward spiral in life and vitality.

And yet, the church Vestry should be wise about saving money and holding some funds in a reserve account for future use or plans. We all should do that in our own personal lives. And it is very difficult for a church that is financially stretched to ever imagine a time when they would have the luxury of putting money away for a "rainy day."

There is another approach that some people on a Vestry will promote. This is a "faith-budget" approach. It sounds like it should be the right thing for a church to advocate. Indeed, a church should walk and budget by faith. In fact, from a certain point of view, every dollar given and spent in a church is given in faith. But a "faith-budget" approach would have only a little bit of money set aside for savings. After all, God pays for what he orders, it is said. But there is ample evidence in Scripture about the need for savings plans, insurance, retirement funding, and the wise use of money. Setting aside a certain amount of money as a reserve is not an indication of a lack of faith or a deeper faith. Saving money is just a good-sense business practice that a church can and should employ.

But how much?
In determining an amount that the church should have set aside in savings, consider these important facts:

- The church is the only non-profit that gathers its donor-base once a week. This means that if the church ever gets into immediate financial danger or crisis, a congregational meeting with its donor base is at most six days away.

- Everyone in your church wants your church to thrive.

- Communications about the financial needs of a congregation are easily drawn up and disseminated.

- Most financial crises are easily addressed, at least initially, by asking people to give.

So how much should the church have in savings? In my view, the church should have 3–4 months of operating cash to use as a buffer. Some Vestry leaders may want to see 5-6 months of reserves to 'fall back on'. Either way, the point is that the church does not need to have 3 *years* worth of money sitting in the bank. Once a financial reserve is in place, the church will not need to panic during low times or a snowstorm when services might need to be cancelled. I do not imagine that any donors would balk at that amount being held in reserve. Many donors would rest assured that their church is acting wisely.

This amount might seem an easy achievement for some churches. The younger and/or smaller churches might never imagine having that kind of security. But every church will need to address this aspect of financial planning and preparation. And, in concert with the Rector, the Vestry will need to be diligent about knowing when to save these funds and, once saved, when to spend them.

I want to add an anecdote from my role as a parish consultant. I have worked with three parishes over the last few years that, financially speaking, seemed solid and strong. They all had good cash reserves. Their annual income was steady but trailing off a bit. But as I studied the week by week life of the congregation, they were dwindling. Their giving base was generous, but they were all aging. Attendance was in a steady decline. And the church was devoid of visitors and families.

In my conversations with each of these Vestries, they knew things had to change for their church to survive. They needed to spend some money on new staff, creative advertising, better music, and other improvements. They needed new life, somehow. And they had the money in the reserve fund to do it all. In fact, one parish had two years' worth of money in a "Rainy Day Fund." One evening, during a Vestry meeting, they were reviewing their declining attendance. They wondered what to do. I advised that they should consider spending some of their savings for some very specific changes and improvements.

"But we can't afford it!" one Vestry member said. And from the current income stream, he was right. Their annual budget was maxed out. "But you have two years of money in reserve," I said. "Yes, but that is our Rainy-Day Fund," said a long-standing member of the church who had been recently elected. "Friends," I said, "it is raining!"

The point is made. *A church can spend itself out of business. We can all see how that could happen. But it is also true that a church can save itself out of business too.*

4. Compensation

As we have seen in other dioceses, the role of the Vestry is to provide for the support of the Rector. This is an essential role, and it certainly cannot fall to the Rector to decide. Your diocese might have a recommended minimum standard that you can reference, but from my experience, it is probably too low. And the Vestry should not expect the Rector to "make a bid" for his/her salary. That puts the spiritual leader in the unwanted role of a negotiator.

There are nine areas of financial compensation that the Vestry should consider. Most of them will be "set" for the Vestry by costs and rates of, for example, health care. Once these costs are established and fixed into an annual budget, then the rest of the compensation can be adjusted according to sound wisdom and financial stewardship.

The nine areas for consideration are these:

1. Salary costs for a full-time Rector

2. Housing allowance

3. Social Security reimbursement

4. Health insurance, vision, dental, etc.

5. Retirement funding

6. Automobile allowance

7. Continuing education

8. Hospitality and Ministry expenses

9. Travel allowance

IX. FINANCIAL CONCERNS

Young churches without a history of clergy compensation might struggle to meet these expenses and be forced to choose which to fund and which to delay. That indeed might be a last resort for the Vestry. And it is often true that clergy are more than willing to forgo these expenses and carry the burden of them personally.

But I believe that the Vestry would be wise to pray about these issues, receive guidance from other Vestries and congregational leaders, and explain these costs to the parish in a winsome way. Most churches want to be as generous as possible with their Rector.

One part of the compensation for clergy is unique to all clergy and often needs further explanation for Vestry members. Currently in the United States of America, there is a special provision of the law that allows clergy to exclude their housing allowance from reportable income, provided that the Vestry specifically designates a portion of their salary for that purpose. Each year as part of the annual budget process, the Vestry should review and approve housing allowances for applicable clergy. Even if housing is provided, there may be a housing allowance for general maintenance and upkeep. This should be reflected in the minutes.

Here is the language from the IRS website:

If you receive as part of your salary (for services as a minister) an amount officially designated (in advance of payment) as a housing allowance, and the amount isn't more than reasonable pay for your services, you can exclude from gross income the lesser of the following amounts:

- *the amount officially designated (in advance of payment) as a housing allowance;*

- *the amount actually used to provide or rent a home; or*

- *the fair market rental value of the home (including furnishings, utilities, garage, etc.).*

The payments officially designated as a housing allowance must be used in the year received.

The Vestry has a responsibility to designate the amount before the tax year in which it is claimed. In other words, it is not retroactive. There is quite a bit of information available on the internet about the Clergy Housing Allowance provision.

While it is a definite financial gain for the minister, it should be remembered that the amount excluded from income taxes has no impact on the church budget; it is just a category of compensation.

See Appendix 6 for a specific tax-exempt housing resolution that can be adapted for use in your congregation.

Awkward Moment

The subject and discussion of money is an awkward moment for the Rector and the Vestry. But it is important to have it. Very important. No minister is working in the church to get rich. None of us do this for money. But if a Vestry is unwilling to have a conversation about the Rector's compensation and do the right thing by him or her, it sends a very discouraging message to the Rector.

To ease the awkwardness of the conversation, I would suggest this pattern of discussion.

- In the Fall, the Sr. Warden and Rector begin a conversation about compensation. The Rector is asked to pray about the needs of his/her family and the level of compensation that he/she receives, keeping in mind the financial strength and age of the congregation.[3] The Rector might take the occasion to speak with a financial planner to assess the financial health of his/her family.

- The Rector and Sr. Warden should have a follow-up meeting before the annual budget is ratified by the Vestry.

- The Vestry and Rector can meet together to discuss the budget, the allocation of funds, the vision for the year ahead, and some of the goals and efforts that will be set.

---

3 Some start-up churches are too young to pay the Rector what would be a "going rate." But in time and with some growth, this should be corrected as soon as possible.

- The Vestry can go into "Executive Session" and ask the Rector to leave the meeting. The Sr. Warden can relate past conversations with the Rector and suggest adjustments to his/her compensation.

How Much?

This is a difficult subject to address because every church will be different in its ability to fund a position as Rector. Some Rectors are bi-vocational, or they work as a volunteer for the church and gain their living through outside employment. Some Rectors are retired and have an income apart from the church budget. Some Rectors need the church to be much more generous with their compensation package because of personal needs. As I say, it is difficult to give guidance on this. There are reports and worksheets that are available online that address the Sr. Pastor's compensation. Often, a diocese might have a suggested "minimum" standard that should be met. In some situations, these standards might be helpful; they are often not.

I have suggested a unique way of "benchmarking" compensation levels in the church for the Rector and for any staff. I honestly cannot remember where I first heard this plan, but it has been very helpful as a way of "getting in the ballpark" regarding compensation for the Rector. The local school system has published salaries and benefit packages for teachers and administrators.

There are "like" categories between the two disciplines of education and ministry. I am not equating the work of one with the work of another, but public school pay scales can be a useful benchmark for Vestry members to consider, adjusted as needed.

5. Facilities

The issue of facilities is very complex within the ACNA. Some parishes have historic buildings and properties. Some have lost such buildings and are in the process of building new spaces. Many of our church plants rent facilities and will be involved in building projects soon. The Vestry does not need to serve as the project manager or real estate agent, but they must be aware of what is going on in this area. They need to know the costs for capital improvements, operational costs, and maintenance needs. They should budget accordingly for them. They must also make sure they are in compliance with local regulations in terms of their facilities and facility usage. One key thing is that there needs to be a clear policy about usage. Are buildings and facilities available for rental and use by outside groups? What protocols govern this process? Facilities should be safe, clean, and in legal compliance for each congregation. By the way, there will be further regulations if there is a columbarium or cemetery on the church grounds. Historical properties will also have their own issues of local compliance and regulation.

Vestries should receive counsel and wisdom from bankers, realtors, and other professionals when it comes to renting, leasing, purchasing, or renovating any facility. It is beyond the scope of this book to give advice or direction other than to say this: your Vestry should seek sound advice and direction.

6. Insurance

The church needs to carry appropriate and reasonable levels of insurance. The Vestry should make sure that this is done. If the church owns property, then there should be appropriate levels of property insurance. There should also be insurance for and a proper inventory of church assets. The church should carry general liability insurance, insurance for any motor vehicles, and directors' and officers' liability insurance. In addition, there will be workers' compensation insurance, health insurance for clergy and staff, and disability insurance. We recommend that each church work with an insurance agent who can put together a full policy to cover all of their needs. The Vestry will ensure that this happens and will generally work on proper risk management.

7. Child Protection

A church is a wonderful family of faith that (usually) tries not to judge people or limit their involvement in any way. In a rush to fill volunteer positions, churches can make the mistake of broadening their appeal and failing to adequately vet the people who sign up to help. It is a sad truth that the warmth and accepting nature of the local church can attract people who are predators or would be inappropriate with children.

Thus, the church, in an effort to protect young children and students, must provide for background checks, certified training, and other protective measures. It is normally true that if a clergy person has been revived by "letters dimissory," they have been fully vetted and released by another diocese. But it is also true that fulfilling the training requirement of every volunteer who ministers or leads children and students is very hard. People just don't want to do it. Yet, it is essential. The Vestry should ensure that the Rector has completed this vetting process for all new volunteers.

This 'need' is hard to even imagine speaking about. As a parish Rector I was very reluctant to bring up the subject. I didn't want our members and visitors to associate our church with the predatory practices of people with twisted minds. At the same time that I was growing this young church I was also growing a young family with four children. As I would go to their schools for parent meetings or 'orientation' meeting for new families, I found that every institution that seeks to teach and nurture children also had programs that were mandatory and advertised as mandatory for all teachers, staff, and volunteers. Not only did this protect the children by training leaders and raising awareness, the public nature of these programs sent a clear and strong message of vigilance to any would-be offenders.

The Vestry has an important role to insure that these kind of 'child-safe' training and awareness programs are provided and made mandatory for all childcare workers, teachers, and volunteers. This is often an on-going task of every diocese and the bishop has clear requirements. The cost of these programs is negligible, but it should be a line item in the annual budget.

8. By-laws and Policies

This is the boring part of the role of the Vestry…until it isn't. If a congregation gets to a point where it is referring to policies and by-laws to prove a point or bolster an argument, it is not usually a good thing. The Vestry should have an ongoing duty to establish, evaluate, and formally review all by-laws and operational policies on a regular basis. Again, it is not exciting work and should usually take place apart from the Vestry's monthly meeting. For example, what is the policy for the use of the building. If the church does not have a clear statement of who can and cannot rent or use the property or facilities, it could be a problem. If one group is allowed to use the building without charge (like a Boy Scout troop) and then another group asks to borrow the facility, what is the policy for usage? If the second group wants to hold a meeting that violates the closely held faith beliefs of the church, how can a church say no?

There are by-laws that could be written proscribing or allowing the building use, for example. By-laws might usually guide the process of searching for a new Rector. By-laws might establish the date, time, and length for the Annual meeting to allow for some flexibility. Most by-laws should allow for the Vestry to vote electronically, via email. The point is that if there is no policy, the church can continue for years and then suddenly be greeted by a problem for which there is no by-law written or the written by-law is outdated.

As I mentioned, creating and maintaining good clear policies and by-laws is not exciting work. And they may never be acutely needed; but when they are, it is good to have them handy and ready.

9. Legal

It is always a good idea to have a lawyer who will either volunteer their time or offer their services at a discount to the parish. There are legal issues that the Vestry needs to be aware of as they work with the Rector as he leads the vision. For example, it might be that the Rector and staff need to have an up-graded copier for the church. That is usually a lease agreement, and the Vestry needs to have comfort that the church is not entering into the wrong or wrongheaded kind of contract. There are person-nel issues that a church is constantly dealing with. In dismissing a key staff person, will the church be subject to legal action for "wrongful termination"?

If the church is going to purchase a piece of land, a lawyer will be needed to look over the documents. This legal function is a key role for some attorney to assume. The traditional name for this role is "Chancellor," and they will often add great value to vestry discussions. If a Chancellor is attending a Vestry meeting, he or she can often be consulted in real time. They have voice but no vote in all matters.

It is a good policy to require that contracts, lease agreements, specific written financial agreements be inspected and approved by the parish attorney. Who is that person in your parish? Do you have a volunteer chancellor, a team of legal professionals, or an attorney on retainer?

10. Banking

Finally, a church needs a very positive and personal relationship with a local bank. There are quite a number of transactions that a church engages in over the course of a month. The number cannot be known, but my guess is that it is larger than an average client or customer of the local bank. Consider all the EFT transactions, checks, auto-drafts, and bill payments that come in and out of the local church on a routine basis. In addition, as mentioned above, a congregation can have a good-sized balance in a savings account or a rainy-day fund (unless it is raining!). All of this is music to the ears of a banker. It is always a good practice for the Rector and the local banker to be on a first-name basis.

In addition, I would often counsel churches to establish a line of credit for emergencies if ever needed. The best time to take out a line of credit, as most bankers and all lawyers will attest, is when you don't need one. It is just a precaution so that the Vestry and the parish can act freely to seize unique opportunities as they might present themselves.

X. BEST PRACTICES

WE HAVE LOOKED at many different issues that a Vestry must address. We have given a quick survey of the governance for the Anglican Church congregation. We have given a brief overview about the role of the Rector and that of the Vestry. But there is a final chapter needed to address a random set of "best practices" that a Vestry and Rector can achieve in their ministry together. These may not be practical in some congregations; they might take time to develop in others. But I think this section might be worth hearty consideration and discussion at the Vestry and Rector level. Whatever can be done to increase the health and strength of this work together should help the overall mission of the church carry and preach the Gospel of Christ.

Here are six best practices (among many that could be contributed by others).

1. Have Effective Meetings

After looking closely at the role and responsibilities of the Vestry, what about the actual Vestry meeting itself? What does it look like to have regular, effective meetings to do the work God has given you to do? The last thing any of us want to do is show up for ineffective meetings that could have simply been emails! I want to talk about some basic guidelines for Vestry meetings, Robert's Rules of Order, and the annual parish meeting.

Who Attends?

Vestry meetings should be held at a regular time and day of the week each month. This allows Vestry members to write it into their schedules. Usually they are held in person, but they can be equally effective through video conferencing. Within the Vestry, there is a Senior Warden and Junior Warden who work closely with the Rector. Appointed officers usually include the treasurer, clerk, and chancellor/lawyer (when needed). Staff or ministry leaders can be invited to give specific reports. The meeting will usually be chaired by the Rector or the Rector's designee (which may often be the Senior Warden). On occasion, the Vestry meeting may need to go into executive session to discuss specifically confidential items. At that time, guests and, perhaps, the Rector, could be asked to leave the room.

Written Agenda

Each Vestry meeting should follow a basic agenda. It is best practice to distribute the agenda and supporting reports/documents in advance. I would recommend that you start on time and end on time—always. There should be someone appointed to take notes and prepare minutes. This is needed for good practice but is also legally necessary. As a corporation, you need accurate records of the Vestry meetings. Various formats for these meetings are common, but I would make two suggestions.

1. Prayer should be a regular and foundational part of the Vestry meeting. As the church leadership takes counsel together, they need the wisdom and guidance of the Lord.

2. The Vestry should be a learning community. Take time for a devotional or read through a book together. This will help set the proper tone and can help immensely in the leadership capacity of the group.

Traditional Agenda

This very traditional method will build the meeting around four "chunks" of business.

1. Approval of the Past Minutes

2. Financial Report(s)

3. Old Business

4. New Business

This can be a sound, reliable approach—especially if prayer and a learning community element makes up the first part of your meeting before these main parts.

Formational Agenda

I came across this format in a helpful resource called *Beyond Business as Usual: Vestry Leadership Development* by Neal Michell. He is a huge advocate of adding a spiritual and learning community element to Vestry meetings. So, his basic agenda is:

1. Formation (in terms of prayer, study, and learning)

2. Information (things that need no discussion or decision, such as upcoming events, etc.)

3. Discussion (things to be processed in community)

4. Decision (things that require a vote of the Vestry followed by the financial reports)

I would encourage each Rector and Vestry to pick a format and stick to it. Having a clear method for how we do our work together will help us to do our work together with efficiency and joy!

Robert's Rules of Order

I would strongly recommend that Vestry meetings generally follow the protocols set up in Robert's Rules of Order. This will help meetings run smoothly and make it easier to record the minutes and keep accurate records of Vestry meetings. I also realize that not everyone is familiar with these rules, so there should be a basic primer at the initial Vestry meeting each year. At the most basic level, this means that areas for decision or vote are introduced by a motion (from the chairperson or a Vestry member). Each motion should receive a second. At that point, the motion is restated by the chairperson and the motion receives any discussion needed. Finally, the chairperson calls for a vote and announces the result. There is more information and finer nuance as part of this parliamentary procedure, but a basic awareness is needed for the work of the Vestry. I would encourage the chairperson to be diligent in leading the group, keeping the group on topic, and allowing for appropriate amounts of discussion and debate. The chairperson should model courtesy and respect with an appropriate balance of relaxed formality.

Voting Frequency

As a rule of thumb, a Vestry should not have many "motions" or "votes" besides approving the minutes (a formality, usually) or accepting the written and oral report from the Treasurer. The Vestry might insist they should approve every contract or agreement that binds the church to a legal agreement. That is certainly appropriate. But the tone of the Vestry meeting should be more information, education, filled with encouragement, updates, advice, and agreement. If the Vestry is voting too often, they are probably micromanaging the role of the Rector. In real terms, and except for very rare occasions, once the budget is set for the year ahead and all Vestry members are clear on the priorities or programs that need to be strengthened or addressed, there really should be very little left to vote on.

Shorter and Fewer Meetings

The length of the meeting of the Vestry will be in inverse proportion to the size of the church. The larger a church is, the shorter the meeting can be.

And the smaller the church, the longer the meeting. Why is this? Because the larger church has programs that are run and overseen by the staff. The Vestry depends on the Rector to develop the quality of the programs. In a small church, a Vestry tend to be very involved in many of the programs.

Is the secret to growing a church then to have shorter and fewer meeting? Well, if shorter and fewer Vestry meetings indicates a widespread ownership of the mission, great lay involvement in leading programs, and engaged pastoral supervision of all program leaders, then, "Yes". Or perhaps, "Probably".

But in any case, a good rule of thumb would be to keep meeting around two hours.

2. Commit to Annual Vestry Training

You will remember one of the early points that we made: a person being nominated, running, elected, or serving on the Vestry may have no idea of what the task entails. I believe this is true of many, many churches and Vestry members.

It would, therefore, be wise to develop a consistent training program to be repeated annually. This training can be part of the annual nomination and election process. Every church would be different in how these things are implemented, but it would be a wise course of action for the Rector to bring some leadership to an annual event.

X. BEST PRACTICES

As mentioned earlier, it is a standard practice for churches to elect members to serve three-year terms. Consideration and an election of these members might occur, for example, in early February. We can imagine a sequence of events that might look like this.

November: Announcement of Annual Meeting Date (early February) and call for nominees to be submitted to task force chair from the Vestry. At the same time, the outgoing members of the Vestry can gather names of likely candidates and staff members to consider.

December: The names that have been suggested or nominated are vetted through the Rector and the church Treasurer. Why? In the case of the Rector, there should be a consideration of any pastoral or spiritual issues that the nominee might be facing. The Rector should know this person, or at least be aware of their attendance and participation in the congregation. The Treasurer should examine the giving record of the nominee to determine if they are committed to sacrificial giving. These two barometers could not be more important for the future health of the Vestry and the decision that will be made.

January: The Rector should host a mandatory meeting (no more than 3 hours needed) at two different times to allow the Vestry nominees to hear what a Vestry does. Candidly, this book would be an excellent pre-meeting gift for each of the nominees. The meeting should cover these topics at a bare minimum.

- What Is the Mission and Means of the Parish Church?

- Overview of Anglican Governance

- What Are the Five Roles of the Rector and Five Roles of the Vestry?

- A Brief Outline of the Diocesan Canons Regarding the Duties of Rector/Vestry

- Review of Annual Year End Financial Statement (or as current as can be)

- What Are Issues Facing the Church for the Next Five Years?

It is reasonable to expect that each of the nominees could, after an interactive presentation, be able to determine whether they are interested in being nominated. If so, they should submit a brief biographical sketch of their life and ministry. Before they leave the meeting, their photograph should be taken. All photographs and biographies should be turned in and published in a leaflet and on-line two weeks prior to the Annual Meeting.

February: The Annual Meeting should accomplish a few things as itemized below. But the most important thing it should accomplish is the election of a new Vestry and a sincere and gracious send-off of the retiring group. Every church will have its own traditions and ways of saying "thank you." Time served as a Vestry member should be sincerely honored. Most people are honored to be elected and will try their utmost to serve well. It is appropriate to offer a gift in thanksgiving for their service.

March: The Vestry can begin its term of meeting for the year soon after the election. Each new Vestry member should receive a copy of the minutes of the previous year and the closing financial statement of the previous year along with other supporting documentation.

It is a traditional practice of the new Vestry members to have a scheduled retreat to get everyone up to speed, share the mission and means of the congregation, and review a "state of the union" presentation by the Rector. Again, this book is designed to be a handy guide for new Vestry members and old alike. Copies of this book should be a standard issue.

It bears repeating again. Each parish has its own unique culture and system of practices and policies. Those elements constitute a congregation's "tradition." Tradition is not to be violated lightly. It can be changed, added to, or altered, but only after prayer, discussion, and deliberation.

3. Revamp the Annual Parish Meeting

Each church will need to make sure their practice in this area is in compliance with their own by-laws and diocesan Canons. It is assumed that diocesan Canons are in compliance with the province. There are usually two key aspects of the annual parish meeting.

First, there is usually an annual report. This looks back over the past year and gives key, clear data. Information such as attendance, membership, and the budget are included. They should be put in proper perspective in light of the history and vision of the parish. Usually this is passed out as a document and available to all members.

Second, as mentioned above, there is usually an election of new Vestry members. As the older class of Vestry members rotate off, new ones are brought on and strong, healthy parish leadership continues. Thanks be to God!

Okay, But When?

The Annual Meeting of the congregation is something that the by-laws of the parish probably dictate should happen. But I think that the Rector and Vestry can be somewhat creative as to *when* it should happen. Many churches hold their annual meeting on a late afternoon on Sunday. Why? Because many churches hold their annual meeting on Sunday afternoon. It is tradition. The time of the meeting is probably not spelled out in the parish by-laws. And Sunday afternoon (or after the last worship service on Sunday) is fine as far as it goes.

However, there is a built-in problem with the time of the traditional Annual Meeting. If you have ever attended one, you will see it immediately. No one goes! Well, only a few attend. When a congregation holds the meeting on Sunday afternoon, chances are that only core members and die-hard members will attend. The new members and families and younger leaders that attend on Sunday morning would probably not flock to a meeting like this. If that is true, the problem becomes apparent right away. The old guard will, by nature and habit, elect old guard members to serve on the Vestry. They will have the best interests of the church in mind, of course. But it is only to be expected that the new

Vestry will end up looking a lot like the voters to attend the meeting.

This practice will unintentionally skew a congregation to have Vestry members that are from only its existing core. But what about younger members and newer attenders?

Consider how a meeting might be held on Sunday morning when the larger body of the church is already there. The budget can be printed and presented to the congregation as a hand-out. Questions can be submitted by email and text during the week. Could the sermon that day be crafted to be a State of the Church or the Rector's Annual Report? Could nominees for Vestry terms be introduced in person to the congregation? Could votes be cast before the offering and collected as part of the offering? If there is a run-off between two candidates, a run-off ballot can be printed and made available the following Sunday during normal worship times.

One obvious objection to this method is qualifying the voters. Only members should vote for the members of the Vestry. We know that. But you might consider that an "honor system" of asking the non-members to not vote would be a sufficient safeguard. If that is untenable, then specific ballots can be handed out only to members of record before the services begin.

In May?

I sent out a few manuscripts of this book to current Rectors to get their opinion and suggestions. After review, one Rector wrote me about the practice of his church regarding the Annual Meeting. He has it in May! Here is what he wrote:

> We moved our annual meeting to May for the simple reason that having the annual meeting in February seemed like switching quarterback and offensive line at half time. February is the middle of the program year. May represents the end of a programmatic season and allows us to celebrate the year, honor the outgoing team, welcome the incoming group of leaders, and THEN go right into the early summer retreat in a season where we're not pressured with Lent, and Holy Week etc. Having our Annual Meeting in May allows us to celebrate how we lived into the vision the previous year.

What ways can the Rector and Vestry imagine including a large percentage of the church? Some congregations have an annual dinner event to draw people to their Annual Meeting. Some invite a guest speaker or a musical group. What was the attendance at the last annual meeting? If it is substantially smaller than your Sunday morning attendance, you are not getting the optimal strength from the event.

4. Put Your WEDCAP On

WEDCAP is a very simple acronym for the main systems of a church. It has been useful for many churches, both large and small. Vestries and Rectors have used this simple acronym as way of laying out the options and opportunities in their congregational ministry. **WEDCAP** stands for **Worship**, **Evangelism**, **Discipleship**, **Communication**, **Administration**, and **Pastoral Ministry**. These are the six main systems for adult ministry that a church needs to develop to stay alive and vibrant. In my opinion, there are certainly *no less* than six systems. And, in my experience, there are not any *more* than six.[1] But to be clear, if there is weakness in any of these, the church will falter or, at best, stall.

But first, let's look at what a congregational system is.

Consider the human body and the marvelous creation it is. It is a marvel and a miracle in itself. But everyone who has taken Biology 101 knows that there are a number of systems in the body that promote health and allow life to function. When one of those systems is compromised, the whole body will suffer. For example, if the circulatory system is not working well because of a weak heart, then the whole body will suffer. The body may not die, at least not right away. But the body will be compromised and subject to infection. Likewise, each living body has

---

1 An important note of clarification. The WEDCAP model refers to the congregation's ministry to adults, not to children and students/youth. Once a Vestry can see the WEDCAP as a sort of lens through which to see the adult ministry life in the parish, the same WEDCAP categories can be applied to the younger members, both children and youth.

a digestive system that needs to be functioning at a high level for us to have energy and life. If the digestive system is shut down or ineffective, the body will suffer.

The **WEDCAP** system applies these same principles to the Body of the local congregation. If any of these six systems are weak, the entire body will suffer. It may not die, at least, not right away. But it also will never thrive. Worse, if any of these systems is not functioning, the Body of the congregation will be susceptible to infection and other opportunistic diseases. Sadly, many Vestries and former Rectors have lived to tell this tale.

A thorough explanation of these six parish systems is beyond the scope of this book. In future writing I will attempt to take a deep dive in each area. But for now, here are the six **WEDCAP** categories.

1. **The Worship Life:** Primarily, a church needs to worship and honor the Lord Jesus Christ. If a church does not worship or does not have the system to support true, hope-filled, inspirational, authentic worship of our Lord, there is little hope that it will survive. It does not have a reason to survive.

2. **The Evangelistic Life:** A church must always be about reaching out to the people and community around it, bringing in new members, and

making an appealing invitation for people to come and experience the life of the church. This is also an essential element.

3. **The Discipleship Life:** A church must also have a strong program and emphasis to teach and train people about HOW to follow Christ in the modern world; how to live a Christ-centered life in the Power of the Holy Spirit.

4. **Communication:** A church must have a well-devised and coordinated plan to speak to all of its members. Through newsletters, announcements, posts, website management, mailings, notices, and internal messages, a congregation needs to be excellent in "getting the word out" to its members.

5. **Administration:** A church must also have a strong and coherent administrative system to account for funds, pay bills, enter into contracts and agreements, set policies, and make plans for its future. Never underestimate the power of good administration.

6. **Pastoral Connection:** Finally, a church must have a plan to provide ministry, services, and pastoral care for its members not only wholly (as in Worship) but individually as in Confirmation, funerals, hospital visitations, prayer and healing ministry, and pastoral counseling.

These are the six systems that make a church work.

The Vestry Is an A-Team: Administration

It might surprise the Rector and Vestry to know why I am introducing the **WEDCAP** idea as a "best practice." *It is because I believe that the Vestry's role is primarily to operate in the area of Administration*. That is the main function of the Vestry, in my opinion. They can and should have an active interest in helping the Rector achieve excellence in the Worship life of the church. They must allow and budget for proper Communication methods in the parish. They should also maintain the church's commitment to Evangelism, Discipleship, Worship, and Pastoral Care. Each of these categories needs to be made strong in order for the church to thrive.

But by nature, the Vestry's role is primarily to assure clear, robust, and accountable leadership in Administration.

If you are reading this and you serve on the Vestry, you might see this as a "demotion," in a way. You never signed up to help in the "Administration" of the church. But I would encourage you to think of Administration as one of the most important systems of the congregation. It is hard to separate it out, just as it would be difficult to separate out the nervous or skeletal system in the human body. But the Vestry task is absolutely critical to the life and health of a congregation. But its role is primarily Administrative in the broadest sense of the word.

To Illustrate: The Library Board

Can I clarify this by an illustration? My father-in-law served faithfully on the local library board. He loved it, and they loved him. He loved to read, and he read voraciously. He cared about helping children to read more. He helped to raise the funds to put a small garden in the back of the library building. He came to library board meetings with an eager heart to help promote reading and books and literature in his community. He served as assistant treasurer for the library and represented the library to the town council when they asked for information. But my father-in-law was not a librarian. He did not know one thing about the Dewey Decimal System. He was keen on computerizing the entire library but knew he didn't know a thing about that either. His attendance at the monthly library board was a regular part of his personal schedule, but so was his weekly trip to the stacks where he would find new books to borrow and read at home.

He never thought that being on the library board meant that he was suddenly in charge of the library. There was a competent and trained librarian in that role. If you had asked him what he did for the library, he would say that he helped it fulfill its mission. Was his role primarily administrative? Yes! And look at all that he could do under that single heading! He was both a reader and an administrative leader on the board.

I hope the application of this analogy is not lost on readers of this book. So, in applying the analogy to the local congregation, it follows that a Vestry member's main activity should not be direct creation or oversight of a program or ministry of Worship or Discipleship. They can and should have an active interest and investment in these areas. But a Vestry should look to the Rector for leadership in areas such as these. The Rector can (and should) look for ideas, interest, passion, and participation from the Vestry. The Rector can and should rely upon the Vestry to provide feedback and guidance. But the members of the congregation should not expect the Vestry to take over the Worship life of the church.

This Is News to Many Vestries

Typically, a Vestry might assume that they are elected to help run the church services and oversee the congregational life in all of its expressions. This is a difficult task to begin with. And for a rotating group of elected volunteers meeting for 2–3 hours a month, it is simply impossible. And in the attempt to do this, to manage all these program and systems, most Vestries will frustrate the Rector and volunteers and gum up the system.

In fact, it is the role of the Rector is to foster health and spiritual strength in each of these six areas. As mentioned, the Rector may involve members of the Vestry for their advice or counsel. He may create a task force to "look into" an area and help him see the reality more clearly. A Rector can bring up any topic or point of discussion at a Vestry meeting. And conversely, a Vestry member should be encouraged to ask any question at a Vestry meeting. But if the Rector were to ask a Vestry member to "fix" a Discipleship program, for example or "take charge of the newsletter" (Communication), he is asking the Vestry member to take on a staff function. And, as mentioned above, the Vestry is not adjunct staff.

This "systems" approach to looking at the entirety of the congregation is a helpful way to see the church as a whole. And, like the human body, the healthier each of the systems are, the healthier the whole of the body is.

Again, this manual is not the place to fully develop this WEDCAP lens. But perhaps this brief overview might help the Vestry understand their role. More will be said in later publications.

5. Annual Vestry Retreat

There are many good reasons to have an annual retreat with a Vestry. It is often a Friday afternoon and all-day Saturday event that is held after the election of the new members. It can be held at any time if there is serious and focused discussion that is needed. A retreat is a sacrosanct time away for the members of the church, who usually see each other in church or at potlucks, to spend some quality time listening to the Lord's work in their life. A Vestry retreat can often have a guest speaker or consultant come and lead the group in some creative thinking or exercise. If there are decisions that need to be made that require deep prayer and discernment, it is a critical event. Many Vestries have done great work over a course of a few years, and they will often credit the retreat wherein they developed trust and heard each other's stories and hopes for the parish.

The agenda or the format for the retreat will be different for each Vestry. Sometimes the retreat will be to cover some heavy topics or deal with difficult issues. Sometimes there is a more celebratory retreat experience. But in any case, the annual retreat will be seen as a necessary investment of time by most of the attenders.

6. Align Vision, Program, and Budget

The last area in this section is perhaps the most difficult to include in a book like this. The process that a congregation goes through to develop a budget is as unique as its size and culture. If we look back at the metaphor of the different kinds of classrooms, we can see this more clearly. For example, a college-size church will have a very formal and scheduled method of determining an annual budget. Staff will be asked to submit goals and plans for the year ahead, an administrator will help them determine the amount of money that it will take to fund that work, and then the staff will "roll up" all these expenses into a unified budget. There are often weeks of meetings and cost-cutting and prioritizing sessions that will give shape to the budget that is presented to the Vestry, voted on, and then given to the congregation.

The small elementary-size church has no formalized program per se. Often they will have a meeting of the Vestry in one month to "get out the budget and see how we are doing." Then a decision is taken to add, subtract, or change the budget allocations. It can be dealt with on a very informal level.

As mentioned, it is difficult to suggest a process for such a wide variety of congregations and sizes. But what can be suggested for each church as a best practice is this: Align the vision, the program, and the budget so that they are all trying to move the church in a unified direction.

I worked with a young leader of a healthy congregation a few years back. He was very outgoing and well-loved within the parish. I followed him through his budgeting processes and frankly, it was a waste of time and effort. He met with his Vestry and told them of the hopes and dreams that he had for the next year. They left the meeting excited to see it all happen. Then he met with some part-time staff and volunteers in a retreat setting and encouraged them to list their own dreams and hopes for their ministry. But there was never any alignment between what the Vestry heard about his goals and what the staff listed as their goals. He affirmed the staff without sharing his plans with them. He also never shared the staff goals with the Vestry. Thus, there was no connection between the work of the staff, the priorities of the Rector, or the funding approved by the Vestry. They just got along the next year; each one doing their own thing, as it were.

It takes some planning and a good deal of coordination, but a church budget that will adequately fund a congregation's vision and the programs in pursuit of that vision is a beautiful thing. If we return to my Taco Truck illustration, when the Rector, staff, and Vestry are all looking through the same front windshield, there is peace and unity! The truck bed is full of the programs and materials that the church needs for its journey. The money spent is not wasted; rather it is aligned with programs and methods that are intended to meet the needs of the people and develop the goals of the church. Year after year, this produces faith and confidence in both our Father in heaven and the leadership of the church. It also produces a unified budget!

The Enemy of the Best

These are just a few of the best practices that I have seen work well in other churches and that I have attempted in my time as Rector. There is no "one-size fits all," to be sure. And I stand by my earlier caveat: your mileage may vary.

But these practices are offered with a hope that Rector and Vestry will act to pursue the best practices.

A church should never settle for mediocrity in what it does and how it does it. Years ago I learned two maxims that have helped shape my ministry as Sr. Rector and now as a church consultant.

The first was this: *"The Good Is the Enemy of the Best."* This means that we often will simply accept "good" in the performance of our duties and ministry and consider that it is good enough. Good enough. That, in my view, should never be the standard for the church of Jesus Christ. I understand that the bottom-line work of the church is not about being great in all things. But surely the church, the oldest continuously renewing organization in the history of the world, deserves more than mediocrity. The church of Jesus Christ deserves our best efforts and practices that will honor God and also build a stable and viable organization.

The second maxim is related to the first: *"The Essence of Strategy Is Sacrifice."* This means that we often need to choose to say no to many things that we could do in favor of doing the one thing that we are called to do. Personally, I have been persuaded that few churches are failing because they are not doing enough. Churches struggle because they are doing too much. Their energies and resources are too scattered among a variety of programs and efforts that involve people's best time and energy.

In other words, the best of Best Practices will often

be fewer practices. A friend of mine saw me in my earlier days of ministry when I was running around as if my hair was on fire. I was doing many, many things in the parish and trying to involve and include as many people as I could to advance the vision of the church that God had given me. I was earnest, to be sure. But I was exhausted too. My friend drew me aside and spoke these memorable words: "David, you can do anything you want, but you cannot do everything you want." Boom! Point made.

XI. A FINAL LOOK

MY WIFE AND I HAVE a kitchen filled with cabinets and drawers for cooking utensils, pots, pans, plates, glasses, flatware, and assorted dishes. Each of the drawers has a special purpose. We try to stay organized that way, as do most families, so that we can find things when we need them.

But we also have what we call a "Junk Drawer." And in speaking to other people about their own kitchen, I think that most everyone has a catch-all drawer like that. And I have discovered that most people call it by the same name: Junk Drawer. It doesn't mean that the items in the drawer are junk. If they were, we would throw them in the trash. But it means that the drawer looks junky because a lot of things go in it that we cannot find a better place for.

With that mind, here is the chapter dedicated to the junk that doesn't fit anywhere else. Some of these statements were mentioned in the course of this book, but they may have been glossed over. But here is a random list of what the Vestry and Rector need to know or to do. These ideas and items are part of the unique Anglican polity that I outlined earlier in the book.

• The members of a congregation never vote on

anything except who is elected to the Vestry. The Vestry votes on everything else. For example, the annual budget is never subject to a vote from the members of the congregation. In the language of Robert's Rules of Order, the Vestry does not "move" the budget for approval by the congregation. The budget is presented.

- A Rector is not a member of the church that he or she leads. This was mentioned early in the book, but it would be easy to overlook. The Rector and other clergy are not members of the congregation. They are members of the diocese.

- The entire staff, clergy and lay, report to and serve at the pleasure of the Rector. He/she can hire and fire members of the staff according to his/her office. (A smart Rector will never take precipitous action, however. Normally, any staff interruptions or dismissals are the subject of serious discussion and prayer at the Vestry level. But the Rector does not need permission to exercise this authority.)

- The Rector does not work for the Vestry. Therefore, the Vestry cannot terminate the Rector. Once a Rector is "installed," the Rector has tenure in the parish. The Vestry might have ongoing conflict and they might hope to terminate the Rector, but they cannot. Many dioceses have Canons that outline a process of resolving conflicts between the Rector and the Vestry. All of them involve consulting with the Bishop. It would be prudent to look at your diocesan Canons for guidance if this situation arises. Pray that a Bishop's intervention is never needed.

- In the case of the Rector's absence, resignation, death, or termination through appropriate channels, the "next in charge" of the congregation is not the Assistant or Associate Rector. It is the Sr. Warden! A lay person, representing the entire Vestry, is placed in the leadership role. Smart Sr. Wardens will immediately call for prayer and ask the Bishop to help appoint an Interim or Acting Rector while a formal search process is conducted.

- Both a church and a non-profit are tax-exempt organizations registered as a 501(c)3 entity. But a church is not a non-profit organization in the same way that a non-profit charity is. They are very different entities and need to be considered as distinct. Consider their funding and development. Most churches have donors who are the main recipients of the ministry of the church; most donors to non-profits are not the target audience for the non-profit. Churches foster personal relationships among donors and between the Rector and donors; donors for charities and non-profits seldom meet. Churches have typically larger donors and fewer of them than the local charity; non-profits seek to have a very large donor base that gives relatively smaller gifts. This is why something like Giving Tuesday is not appropriate for the local church.

- People who serve on a Vestry are typically not chosen because they have unique gifts and abilities that are needed in the church. There are exceptions to this, but they are exceptions. The best way to find people who have particular gifts and abilities that might be needed is to recruit them. Often an unexpected resignation from the Vestry can allow the Vestry the occasion to ask, "What kind of person do we need to serve with us?" The Sr. Warden or the Rector can recruit the specific person to be elected to fulfill the unexpired term of the resigned.

- The larger the church, the fewer ways it feels connected to the diocese. The smaller the church, the more it relies upon the programs and resources that a diocese can provide. Consequently, the larger the church the less it feels that the diocese provides anything useful.

- I mentioned earlier that a Rector should never surprise a Vestry with a brand-new idea or a quick and sudden turn. This is practical wisdom from years of leading Vestry meetings. But if it is unwise to surprise a Vestry with new ideas that need quick action, it is nearly a sin to surprise a Senior Warden at a Vestry meeting!

I am sure there are many other items that are candidates for this "Junk Drawer." They can be added in future editions of this manual.

Conclusion

This book has been filled with ideas and concepts that will fit many congregations, their Rectors, and their Vestry. Most Rectors will want to adapt or adopt parts of this book for discussion and development within the context of a Vestry meeting or as the subject of a Vestry retreat. I hope this book has been helpful to you. As we are able, LeaderWorks will update this book year by year and produce a newly revised edition for each year.

You are most welcome to send in suggestions, corrections, or points that should be clarified. Our hope is that we can collect some of the best resources for leaders and Vestries and turn them into useful books and guides.

Some of the material in the Appendix will not impact every church; perhaps it will be useful to only a few. But we include it in order to help every church at any age or stage. If you have suggestions for future Appendices, please let me know: David@Leaderworks.org

STARTING
NEW VESTRIES

THERE ARE NOT A LOT OF RESOURCES out there focused on best practices for Vestries. That's part of why I have put this book together. By the way, some of the resources that do exist and are helpful are listed in Appendix 3. I want to take a moment to address a unique situation. The term "Vestry" is a fairly old term. Centuries ago in the Church of England, the Vestry was a room on the church grounds. This is the room where the clergy would vest prior to the service. Parish leadership meetings were held in this room. Over time the name of the room and the body of the parish leadership merged and so the body of parish leadership is now known as the Vestry. Resources are written about these Vestries. There are guidelines for electing new Vestry members for 3-year terms of service.

In the ACNA, church planting has been a key and ongoing emphasis in our movement. But, to my knowledge, there are no resources written for starting Vestries. This means that many churches are dealing with new structures and new members. What does establishing a new Vestry look like for them? Is it reasonable to expect someone to commit to a 3-year term of service when the church itself is only 9 months old? This becomes particularly difficult when one realizes that some of the key leadership traits for healthy, pioneering church planting may not necessarily overlap with ideal Vestry member traits for overseeing the temporal matters of the parish. Beyond that, the very process of Vestry elections may be unhelpful for new congregations coming together as a new community. Plus, you don't want to elect an entire Vestry all at once on the first year since, by design, Vestry members have staggered terms. So, what should we do? I spoke with a young church planter. Here is what they did, and it seems like a great way forward. This was done in ADOTS under the purview of the Archbishop. So, it is legit!

Initially, the duties of the Vestry should be overseen by a mission board appointed by the sponsoring church or sponsoring diocese. They should fulfill the role of the Vestry as the church is becoming established. In some parachute scenarios, the church planter may even be employed as a missioner of the diocese and the church plant function under their administrative "cover." At some point the church will begin to grow and be ready to formalize membership. At that point, as the bishop to appoint the first group of Vestry members who will comprise approximately 1/3 of the anticipated full Vestry body. The mission board and the missioner will be aware of those committed to the new church and gifted for this specific work. Ask the Bishop to appoint them as the first Vestry members. If you anticipate a 9-person Vestry, then appoint the first three. Then, the next year elect three more and so on and so forth. This allows you to ensure the right first Vestry members and begins the process that will result in staggered Vestry member terms. It also helps keep the focus on mission and planting rather than the unfortunate popularity dynamics of a Vestry election. The last thing a new church needs is for people to leave with hurt feelings of frustration over the first Vestry election. Instead, appoint the first group of Vestry members and begin to teach the congregation about the role of the Rector, the role of the Vestry, and proper Anglican governance. Everyone needs to be able to trust that the temporal (especially financial) matters are being attended to and are above reproach, but you don't have to pretend that a two-year-old mission has the established Vestry life of a decades-old church. This group can be working alongside a launch team or core team.

SEARCH PROCESS OVERVIEW

THROUGHOUT THIS VESTRY GUIDEBOOK we have assumed that healthy churches have healthy leadership from healthy Rectors and healthy Vestries! But there is a unique scenario that some Vestries will encounter. Many Vestries will be part of a Rector search process. Some of these may be due to unfortunate circumstances, but many more will be natural as clergy retire or are called to other work. What does it mean to be on the Vestry during a Rector search? How does this change the dynamics of leadership? What should the Vestry do during this time, and what should they avoid in order to make sure that the new Rector has a proper scope and potential for leadership? On the one hand, I want to simply put this on your radar. In the event of a Rector search, the leadership mantle will pass to the Vestry as they work with the Bishop and diocesan officials. This will be a key moment for prayer, discernment, and the proper exercise of leadership. Vestry members will need to be honest about where they are as a congregation and what needs they have going forward consistent with the overall vision of the church—not just the outgoing Rector, current Vestry, or incoming Rector—but there needs to be an overall vision for the church. Further, you should know that in the absence of the Rector, the Senior Warden is the chief local ecclesiastical authority until the Bishop appoints a priest-in-charge, interim Rector, or installs the new Rector. If you are considering accepting the additional responsibility within the Vestry of serving as Senior Warden, know that this may be part of the job.

So, what should you do? First, reach out for help. Your Bishop and diocesan office will have resources for you. The first step will be to form a search committee. I would recommend that this be a different group than the acting Vestry. There will be Vestry representation (and warden representation), but it should have a cross-section of key leaders in the congregation. You will need to gather basic information about the state of the parish and its vision. Hopefully, these can be compiled from the annual reports and the vision and values are not simply on paper or stored in a file, but are living, known realities by everyone on the Vestry and in the parish already. The search committee will prepare a parish profile and Rector description and begin receiving applications. Be patient and prayerful. It will take time to receive and vet resumes. You will begin narrowing the resumes down for further conversation. You will narrow it again to begin checking resumes and doing visits. It will continue to be filtered down further until it becomes apparent who God is calling to become the next Rector. They will need the consent of the Bishop, recommendation of the search committee, and approval of the Vestry. By the way, this can't be the sole focus of the congregation. The vision cannot go on autopilot and should not be solely dependent on the Rector. Mission and ministry must go on during the search and be ready for the arrival of the new Rector. The Vestry will be called on in extraordinary ways during this season to model patience, prayerfulness, and wisdom. The Vestry will need to be both appropriately urgent and a steady, non-anxious presence. The Vestry should also be eager and expectant for the new things that God is doing in their midst and the next phase of their congregational life together. Be flexible and welcoming when the new Rector arrives and know that you have done a good and vital work over and above the normal call of duty for Vestry members!

THE RECTOR'S EVALUATION

I WANT TO GIVE SOME hard-earned advice in the area of evaluation of the Rector. I say that it is hard-earned advice because I made some serious mistakes about the process of evaluation that nearly derailed my ministry at Christ Church. I was the Rector and Sr. Pastor at Christ Church for 31 years. I loved it all. And I had 30 years of Vestry meetings that were amazing, stellar, and exciting. And I had one year of very difficult meetings that centered around the process of evaluation.

All staff can and should be evaluated by their supervisor or their direct reports. In small churches, this can be done over a cup of coffee and a conversation about ministry effectiveness. The larger the church grows, the more formal this process will become. As staff are called and hired to serve the church in many areas of ministry, the Rector must provide a way of helping the staff realize their calling and use their gifts and, at the same time, advance the mission of the local congregation. There are standard business practices about personnel practices and staff evaluation that can be adapted for use by the church. Once again, this is something that goes in the back of the truck. It is the way that the Rector provides for the congregation; by developing a well-functioning and balanced team of leaders to serve the greater mission of the church.

But when it comes to evaluating the Rector, I would add two things:

1. It should be done. The Rector really does need to know how he/she is doing from the viewpoint of the congregation and the goals and objectives of the parish. Is the congregation growing? Are the staff well-trained? Are the pastoral needs of the congregation being met? Are sermons preached that are cogent, thoughtful, and biblically sound? So, yes, there is a need for a good, serious, evaluation.

2. There is no one to do it. The people that the Vestry would naturally turn to are the Wardens of the church, maybe in conjunction with others in the parish. They are certainly close enough to the Rector's heart and ministry life that they would be useful. But they should *not* do it; at least not fully. They cannot know the activity and heartbeat of the Rector. They cannot judge the actions and methods he/she uses to lead the church. Many Wardens come from the field of business where results are quantified, and metrics are established. But this is not the language of ministry. Ministry is about presence. Ministry is about prayer and practices to keep the parish engaged and on mission of the church.

Can the Bishop evaluate the Rector? This is a great step in the right direction because only the Bishop can know the spiritual aspects of the role of Rector. Ideally, the Bishop should know the heartbeat of the

Rector and the personal and spiritual morale that he or she has. That might be possible, but sadly, it is only rarely so. The Bishop has a full plate of duties and responsibilities and in some sense, he or she is also removed from the real heartbeat of the Rector.

So, in a sense, it is a puzzle. The Vestry can but should not; the Bishop should but cannot. But it is nevertheless important to do.

This is the quandary I found myself in during the one rough patch of ministry at Christ Church. The Wardens could have been the ones to evaluate me, I agree. But since neither of them is in ministry, they did not know the language or the theological realities that the Rector has to juggle. These were good men of God, and I know that their intentions were very honorable. But in the process of the evaluation, they began to tell me what I should be doing on a day by day basis. They suggested that I start to quantify my ministry in terms of how many people I could bring in to church vs. how many people were moving into the neighborhood. They wanted a measurable goal and a set of numbers that would produce something tangible. They wanted a score-sheet. They imagined that there were right and effective mechanics in ministry that simply aren't there; or at least should be assumed to be there.

As I say, these were good and godly men, but they worked in the world of business and simply did not understand the unique role of the Rector. Candidly, I discovered that I was a sinful rebel too. I did not like having someone hold a measuring stick up to my ministry. These men might remember and tell the account differently, but from my perspective I felt every bit a sinner. I was wanting some perspective and reflection on my ministry, but when I started to engage others, I discovered that I really didn't!

And I could not ask the Bishop to interfere with our church and set aside his busy schedule and come spend three hours with me. He would have been willing to do it, but it would not have been sustainable.

So, how did I do this annual evaluation? The way I settled this issue was to blend everything together into a coherent plan that I followed for the next few years. Here is what I did:

I wrote a 4–5 page assessment of my role as Rector answering a series of questions having to do with the culture of the parish, our mission, how I felt the Spirit of God leading me, my preaching life, my prayer life, my family life, and my personal habits and known sins of omission and commission.

Then I summarized this long paper into an appropriate one-page summary for the two Wardens and my Bishop. I held a one-hour phone call with the Bishop to review my long paper, and I asked for his advice and counsel and prayer. Then I reviewed the shorter paper with the Wardens and then summarized the Bishop's advice to me verbally.

The last step was to put this on the agenda as an item for discussion at the Vestry meeting. I gave a redacted and edited version of the one-page paper to the Vestry and summarized the process. I also included a few "next steps" that I would seek as a minister of the Gospel.

I hope this account of this thorny issue will help future Vestry and Rector relationships. Moreover, I hope that both the Rector and Vestry will see the important aspects of evaluation of this most unique role within the congregation. It would be a very helpful exercise for the Rector and the Wardens to talk about the issue of the Rector's evaluation and set out a formal, written, mutually agreed upon program of reflection, discussion, and evaluation and then to annually edit and improve it over time.

CANONS EVERY VESTRY SHOULD KNOW

THE CONSTITUTION AND CANONS of the Anglican Church in North America have clear directions for the primacy of the local congregation and vestries. These are the most pertinent items according to the Constitution and Canons of the Anglican Church in North America that were ratified by the Inaugural Provincial Assembly, June 2009 and amended by the fifth Provincial Assembly, June 2019.[1]

From the Constitution:

Article III: The Mission of the Province
1. The mission of the Province is to extend the Kingdom of God by so presenting Jesus Christ in the power of the Holy Spirit that people everywhere will come to put their trust in God through Him, know Him as Savior and serve Him as Lord in the fellowship of the Church. The chief agents of this mission to extend the Kingdom of God are the people of God.

Article IV: The Structure of the Province
1. The fundamental agency of mission in the Province is the local congregation.

Article XII: Ownership of Property
All church property, both real and personal, owned by each member congregation now and in the

future is and shall be solely and exclusively owned by each member congregation and shall not be subject to any trust interest in favor of the Province or any other claim of ownership arising out of the canon law of this Province. Where property is held in a different manner by any diocese or grouping, such ownership shall be preserved.

From the Canons:

Title I: Canon 6 – *Of Congregations*
Section 1 – *Concerning Congregational Mission*

The fundamental agency of the mission of the Church to extend the Kingdom of God is the local congregation. The chief agents of this mission are the people of God.

Section 2 – *Concerning Congregations*

A congregation in this Church is a gathered group of Christians who have organized and function in accordance with the canons of this Church attached to a diocese and under the oversight of a Bishop. Every congregation of the Church belongs to the Church by union with a Diocese of the Church or through a Diocese-in-Formation. A congregation of this Church is a gathering where the pure Word of God is preached and the sacraments are duly administered according to Christ's ordinance (Article XIX).

Section 3 – *Concerning Organization*

Every congregation shall be established in accordance with the laws of the State or jurisdiction where situated, shall handle its own finances, and shall carry insurance coverage in amounts specified by its Diocese, except in those Dioceses with constitutional or canonical provisions to the contrary.

Section 4 – *Concerning Congregational Clergy and Lay Employees*

1. No Rector may be called to or dismissed from a congregation without the consent of the Bishop. No other clergy may be called or dismissed from a congregation without consultation with the Bishop. A diocese may adopt canons not in conflict with this section.

2. All assistant clergy and lay employees of the congregation shall serve under the direction of and at the pleasure of the Rector except as may be otherwise provided under local law.

Section 5 – *Concerning Governing Boards*

There shall be a governing board of each congregation, often known as the vestry, which is chosen and serves according to applicable laws, diocesan canons, and the congregational by-laws. The Presbyter in charge of the congregation shall always be a member of the governing board and its presiding officer except as provided by diocesan canon. The governing board is responsible for the temporalities of the congregation and, except where otherwise provided by canon, supports the clergy in the spiritual leadership of the congregation.

Section 6 – *Concerning Property Ownership*

All congregational property, real and personal, owned by a member congregation is and shall be solely and exclusively owned by the congregation and shall not be subject to any trust in favor of the Province or other claim of ownership arising out of the canon law of the Church; neither may any Diocese assert any such claim over the property of any of its congregations without the express written consent of the congregation. Where property is held in a different manner by any Diocese or grouping, such ownership shall be preserved.

Canon 9 – Of Finances
Section 1 – *Concerning the Tithe*

The biblical tithe is the minimum standard of giving to support the Mission of the Church and should be taught and encouraged at every level in the Church.

Canon 10 – Of the Laity
Section 3 – *Concerning Membership in the Church*

Membership in the Church requires that a person has received the Sacrament of Baptism with water in the Name of the Father, and of the Son, and of the Holy Spirit, and that such a person be accepted as a member of the Church by a congregation of this Church in compliance with the Constitution of the Church. Such a person is a baptized member of the Church. A confirmed member is a baptized member who has been confirmed or received by a Bishop of the Church. Dioceses and congregations may establish the norm and standards for membership in good standing.

Title III: Canon 7 – Of Rectors and Other Congregation Clergy

Norms for the calling, duties and support of Rectors and other Clergy, and the dissolution of a pastoral relation shall be provided by each Diocese. Rectors shall be domiciled in the diocese to which their congregation belongs.

WHAT IS A MEMBER?

AS I HAVE CONSULTED with many congregations during their startup phase, one key ingredient often is missing. In the rush and pace to get the church operational or keep early momentum going, there is often no definition of what a member is. This is often dismissed as being too legalistic or too old-school. It is also imagined that people don't join organizations anymore. Membership is nearly meaningless, some say.

I think I understand why. Some leaders tell me there is no need. "We are all one family and people are choosing to associate with us with their attendance. We don't want to be that kind of church that has more members than attenders." I understand this line of thinking. However, in this section I want to offer a reason why membership is important and how, with some creative planning, members can be enlisted to engage the mission of the church.

Has Membership Lost Its Value?

Membership in most organizations often serves the needs of the organization first. This is true of a country club, a fitness center, or a homeowner's association. There are often dues or fees incurred in belonging to the organization that form the budget of the organization. Did you know, for example, that only 18% of people who belong to a gym actually go to the gym. And it might be even less than that.

Some studies have shown that 14% of the people who say they go to work out at the gym really do not go at all!

We do not want our churches to be that sparsely attended. The Christian faith is not a "membership" faith at all. And it is easy to see how a church can grow and, without engaging its membership for mission, become bloated with people who seldom attend or who attend as spectators. There is a broad pathway to inactivity and lax commitment. In fact, it is a constant effort to keep Christians "in shape" and exercising their faith. The Apostle Paul's reminder to Timothy to "fan into flame" the faith he had received should alert us to this truth.

Everyone would agree that attendance is better than membership; at least it is a more meaningful measure of the health of a congregation and its commitment to mission. But if a church does not have a clear form of membership, it has no defined body of believers. Then, if there is no common definition of membership, a church is a group of attenders. If there are no members, how can a church body move or agree to move in a particular direction.

This actually goes back to an Anglican Third Way that I mentioned above. A congregational approach to church governance can afford to have a very open understanding of membership. Members and attenders have little participation in the direction or vision life of a church body. Decisions about that are made at the Elder Board level, in the case of a Bible Church, for example. And membership can easily be bloated in the hierarchical type of church as we have seen. The maintenance of committees, positions, titles, and trappings sometimes can de-emphasize the role of mission in the life of each member. The "Seven Sisters" of mainline denominationalism prove this point.

But the Anglican Way is essentially a bridge between these two types of churches. There are leaders at the Vestry level that have a voice and vote about the vision and direction of a congregation. They take on the role of an Elder Board in this way. And yet, they rotate on and off, appointed to the Vestry by election. A congregational vote occurs and, by faith and hope, the leaders that are chosen to help set and maintain a direction are appointed to this role after they are elected.

In the Anglican Way of church governance, there can be no election or ratification of Vestry members because there is no definition of who can vote! Unless there is some agreed-upon understanding of a membership, no one can join a church! There is nothing to join! And if the church goes through a succession plan (as they all will) how will a new person be chosen? By whom? The Vestry? Well, how are they chosen? Who voted them into the office?

Further, when the church goes to a bank to secure

a loan for a piece of property, the bank officers are going to want to see some proof of strength. They will want to see cash balances in the bank. They may want to see a history of budgets and income. The will most certainly ask for attendance history. But they will also ask a very relevant question: How many members does the church have?

What if, instead of tossing out the entire category, a congregation sought to redeem the role and responsibility of membership from its old-fashioned connotations?

Membership Should Mean Mission

Some of the churches think about membership as a high-bar of commitment, not a low-bar for inclusion. They are not looking for warm bodies or pledge cards; they are looking for engagement. They use the idea of membership as an opportunity to teach the values of the congregation and invite people to become active missionaries in their own lives. In these churches, new member classes or orientation events are held routinely. Vestry and staff are present to welcome and provide hospitality. The Rector is prepared to speak and explain the church's vision and what is expected from new members. This way, new attenders can see and know the mission-purpose up front. They can "sign-on," if you will, and learn how they can be involved, participate, and support the congregation. This new member event is a time of engagement.

APPENDIX 5

The congregation then sees its members not as dues-paying units, but as members of a body. This operating idea from the New Testament seems to strongly suggest that some kind of attachment or participation in a large body is the birthright of any Christian. If they are not engaged in the life of the church, then they are not fully members of the Body of Christ.

Membership, for all of its old-fashioned connotations, is important if for only one reason: members elect a Vestry to serve a term of office to work with the Rector to facilitate the growth of the church and its mission.

FORMS, RESOLUTIONS, AND RESOURCES

Benevolence Fund

WHEREAS, The Reverend .... , an ordained minister, serves .... Church in the Diocese of ..., STATE in the performance of sacerdotal functions and in the conduct of religious worship, and

WHEREAS, ... Church provides a Benevolence Fund to be administered by the Rector, and under the monthly review of the Treasurer it is hereby

RESOLVED, that the Benevolence Fund is to be used for charitable purposes as defined by the IRS as "relief of the poor and distressed or of the underprivileged." Needy is defined in Treasury Regulation 1.170A-4A(b)(2)(ii)(D) as being "a person who lacks the necessities of life, involving physical, mental, or emotional well-being, as a result of poverty or temporary distress. Examples of needy persons include a person who is financially impoverished as a result of low income and lack of financial resources, a person who temporarily lacks food or shelter (and the means to provide for it), a person who is the victim of a natural disaster (such as fire or flood), a person who is the victim of a civil disaster (such as a civil disturbance), [and] a person who is temporarily not self-sufficient **as a result of a sudden and severe personal or f**amily crisis (such as a person who is the victim of a crime of violence or who has been physically abused)."

_____   _____

Senior Warden ... Church   Date

Tax Exempt Housing Resolution for Ordained Anglican Clergy

WHEREAS, The Reverend ..., an ordained minister, serves ... Church in the Diocese ... in the performance of sacerdotal functions and in the conduct of religious worship, and

WHEREAS, ... Church does not provide a residence for The Reverend ..., it is hereby

RESOLVED, that the total compensation paid to the Reverend ... for the period from January 1, 20XX and ending December 31, 20XX, includes an annual payment $X payable at $X per month that is designated as a parsonage allowance within the meaning of that term as used in Section 107 of the Internal Revenue Code as amended.

FURTHER RESOURCES

LEADERWORKS IN A NON-PROFIT ministry that helps leaders do their work. It is our hope that this book and appendix has been helpful to you. It will be updated on an annual basis, so stay tuned to LeaderWorks for further updates in new editions.

I am including below various references, webpages, resources that we consulted while writing this book.

If LeaderWorks can be of service to any Rector or Vestry, please be in touch with me via our website listed below.

Websites

Leaderworks.org

Theevergreenproject.org

AnglicanCompass.com

AnglicanChurch.net

Churchlawandtax.com

Crown.org

Books

Canoeing the Mountains by Tod Bolsinger

The Coming Revolution in Church Economics by Mark DeYmaz

A Failure of Nerve by Edwin H. Friedman

APPENDIX 7

Our Character at Work by Todd D. Hunter

Death by Meeting by Patrick Lencioni

The Trellis and the Vine: The Ministry Mind-Shift That Changes Everything by Colin Marshall and Tony Payne

Beyond Business as Usual: Vestry Leadership Development by Neal O. Michell

A Spirituality of Fundraising by Henri J. M. Nouwen

Robert's Rules of Order

Giving Up by David Roseberry

Finance for Nonfinancial Managers by Gene Siciliano

Next: Pastoral Succession That Works by William Vanderbloemen and Warren Bird

Search: The Pastoral Search Committee Handbook by William Vanderbloemen

The Vestry Handbook by Christopher L. Webber

THE REV. DAVID H. ROSEBERRY

was ordained in 1983 as a priest and has served in Christian ministry since then. He is now the Executive Director of LeaderWorks whose mission is to help leaders do their work. He is a key leader and influencer in the Anglican Church in North America and LeaderWorks publishes the popular Anglican website known as Anglican Pastor. His first book "Giving Up" was widely read in the ACNA and became the impetus for a Province wide program for Generosity and Stewardship training called "The Evergreen Project". He is now working as a full-time writer, coach, consultant, and kickstarter in ACNA. He lives with his wife Fran in Plano, Texas and has four children and five grandchildren.

The Rector and the Vestry is his second book.

The purpose of this book is to lay out, as best I can, the unique relationship between the Rector and the Vestry. The connection and support between the Rector and the Vestry is critical for any ministry or mission to succeed.

LeaderWorks is the non-profit ministry that I began in 2016 when I left the parish of Christ Church. My purpose is to help leaders do their work and to that end, I hope this book will be helpful.

If I may be of help to you and your organization, please do not hesitate to contact me at David@LeaderWorks.org.

Stay in touch with this work at LeaderWorks.org and at our publishing arm AnglicanCompass.com.

 LEADERWORKS

Made in United States
Orlando, FL
06 September 2022

22089115R10118